Praise for *Derailed*

"Roseman's self-disclosures are refreshingly profound. His memoir soberly describes how he avoided being brought down by the negative situational power of the California prison system by being proactive and consciously avoiding the institutional boredom of prison as well as prison dehumanization. The Lucifer Effect, about which I've written, passed over him; Mark's transformational skills enabled him to remain a good guy."

> —Philip Zimbardo, Professor Emeritus of Psychology, Stanford University; creator of the Stanford Prison Experiment; and author of *The Lucifer Effect: Understanding How Good People Turn Evil*

"The motto of the American criminal justice system is 'Equal Justice under the Law,' but sadly, the reality for many decades has not matched the blindfolded lady holding a scale. There is one form of justice for the wealthy, the famous, the well-connected, and those from the upper socioeconomic strata and something qualitatively different for the poor or middle class, who comprise 99.9 percent of the American population. Mark Roseman's detailed recollection of his experiences with the penal system highlights this disparity in many facets. I urge those who are genuinely concerned with inequities in the administration of criminal justice to read his work carefully."

> —Alan I. Bigel, PhD, Professor of Constitutional Law, University of Wisconsin–La Crosse

"Using the incidents and stories from his own experience, Mark Roseman provides us with a window into prison culture that is startling in detail, both jolting and riveting in its description. It opens a world lived in by millions of Americans and yet a world hidden from the notice of the majority. It showed me how what we don't know about the American prison system leads to public toleration of values and practices that, in many ways, betray our ideals."

> —Cathy A. Small, PhD, Professor, Department of Anthropology, Northern Arizona University

D1603874

"Roseman's fascinating and unique account of incarceration in California avoids the clichés of many prison exposés. He shows how state and federal efforts at prison reform have fallen short. His descriptions of patterns of communication, domination, sex, trust/mistrust, and respect/disrespect among prisoners is vivid and disturbing. Roseman honestly addresses the pervasiveness of racial discrimination in the prison system and decries the bleak opportunities post-prison life offers to ex-cons."

—Charles Jaret, Professor Emeritus, Department of Sociology, Georgia State University

"Those of us who are adventuresome and curious often make great efforts to travel to primitive cultures to immerse ourselves in their unique customs, foods, and language. Why not experience this right here on American soil? Mark Roseman's *Derailed* is a compelling account of his two-year prison experience. Roseman, a middle-class lawyer, served time in prison as a result of poor judgments that could have been made by many of us. If you think prison is for others, read this book and then think again!"

—Sandra Haber, PhD, Fellow, American Psychological Association

"This is an important book that needs to be read. It skillfully alternates between the shocking real and mind-boggling surreal of life inside California prisons today. Written unselfishly, with simple, heartfelt, and compelling truth by a former prisoner, it alerts all of us to the evil reality of our modern prisons—places that do far more harm than 'rehabilitation.'"

—Martin J. Silverman, public policy speaker and blogger, retired attorney, marketing director, and public speaking coach

Derailed

Derailed

How Being a Lawyer Taught Me
to Survive in Prison

Mark E. Roseman, JD

OPEN GATE PUBLISHERS

Open Gate Publishers
9000 Crow Canyon Road, #505
Danville, CA 94506
www.opengatepublishers.com

Quantity sales. Special discounts are available on quantity purchases by corporations, associations, and others. For details, contact the "Special Sales Department" at the address above.

Orders by US trade bookstores and wholesalers. Please contact BCH: (800) 431-1579 or visit www.bookch.com for details.

Printed in the United States of America

Cataloging-in-Publication Data

Roseman, Mark E., 1949- author.
    Derailed : how being a lawyer taught me to survive in
prison / Mark E. Roseman. -- First edition.
    pages cm
    Includes bibliographical references and index.
    LCCN 2016911468
    ISBN 978-0-9972341-3-8 (pbk)
    ISBN 978-0-9972341-4-5 (ebook)

    1. Roseman, Mark E., 1949- 2. Prisoners--United
States--Biography. 3. Prisoners--United States--Life
skills guides. 4. Imprisonment--United States.
5. Criminal justice, Administration of--United States.
6. Autobiographies.   I. Title.

HV9468.R67A3 2016   365'.6092
QBI16-900023 First Edition

20 19 18 17 16   10 9 8 7 6 5 4 3 2 1

To my mother, Sylvia M. Roseman,
and to my late father, Abraham "Hesh" Roseman

*As I walked out the door
toward the gate that would
lead to my freedom, I knew
if I didn't leave my bitterness and
hatred behind, I'd still be in prison.*

—Nelson Mandela

Contents

Foreword

I'VE HAD THE PLEASURE of knowing Mark Roseman for almost two decades. We met when he was an attorney and advocate for adult survivors of childhood sexual abuse within the Catholic church, and he was seeking the advice of a psychologist regarding the emotional aspects of abuse. As I talked with Mark at our first meeting, I was impressed with his attention to detail and his integrity.

At that time, his then-wife and law partner, Melanie Blum, was also gaining fame as an attorney, eventually winning a huge settlement for the patients she represented in the UCI fertility clinic scandal.

Mark and Melanie seemed to be living the good life. However, as I would learn later, Mark had a tendency to avoid dealing with business matters that didn't interest him or that he disliked. And unfortunately, his reluctance to deal directly with the "money" side of his law practice—leaving all the financial aspects in his wife's experienced hands—would prove to be his undoing.

Not long after I met him, he and Melanie were accused of misappropriating funds from the settlements they received on their clients' behalf. By then, their marriage had already dissolved.

Mark fully intended to mount a vigorous defense, laying the blame on his wife. However, when he came face-to-face with the victims who were defrauded and heard how they were wronged by the conduct of his firm, he decided to "do the right thing": he accepted his share of responsibility and struck a plea bargain in his case.

When I heard that he would be going to prison, I couldn't imagine how someone like Mark would handle prison life. Needless to say, it was difficult, but his attention to detail (which helped him remember all the unwritten rules of the prison yard) and his sense of humor helped him adapt.

He learned to live every second of his incarceration under the aegis of two "commandments" that he was lucky to receive early on: (1) "Be invisible" (do not make eye contact with anyone, do not cross the clear racial and ethnic boundaries, do not have prolonged interactions with staff, etc.), and (2) "Do the time; don't let the time do you" (monitor your most self-destructive reactions to being in the penal system and manage those reactions closely and carefully).

All that, and much, much more, is the story that Mark tells in this book. He takes you with him on one of life's least predictable journeys and invites you to see how his experience impacted him, how he learned to cope with the journey, and how he managed to survive the trip. You'll have a chance to share experiences that you may never have contemplated and see how, for Mark, having gone to law school played a monumental role in his survival and successful re-entry into life on the outside.

Although Mark's initial goal was to not let prison change him, he is most certainly different now. He has a greater appreciation for life, he trusts his gut more, and he's much less likely to let anyone get away with half-truths. He has also become a passionate advocate for prison reform.

As you read his story, you will come to understand how appreciative I am to be Mark's long-term friend and colleague.

Steven A. Frankel, PhD, JD

Preface

This place is filled with brooding babies. I feel as though I spend my days in a dissociative state. If I touch down to my current reality, I am subject to rapid panic attacks that are very uncomfortable.

—*Letter to a friend, August 2004*

W HAT'S LIFE IN PRISON like? Is prison dangerous? What is the food like? Is there rampant sex and rape? These are some of the questions I heard during my years inside, and since.

People are naturally curious about prison since they're familiar with the lore from books and articles, plays, and the news. One of Tennessee Williams's first full-length plays, *Not about Nightingales* (1938), was based on a newspaper article reporting that four Pennsylvania inmates were roasted alive by prison officials in a punitive boiler room—and that's just the tip of the iceberg in terms of the literature inspired by news from inside.[1]

When I think back to the time I spent inside, memories swirl in my mind. Flash!—I'm working as a bathroom orderly, being trained by an inmate named Juan to wash toilets, sinks, urinals, and mirrors. Juan took his job seriously and without humor and taught me the universal rule: every prison bathroom has a spitting toilet that's never used for shitting. No one wants to associate with bathroom fixtures that have been spat upon. In cells shared by two men, there's one toilet and one sink, and the spitting rule is modified; cellmates decide which fixture is for spitting. To be honest, I never understood the compulsive need to spit, and such conversations became a comical routine I kept to myself.

When I was sentenced to serve four years (though I actually served half that time), I had no idea what to expect. I was a Jewish lawyer, a fact that I learned during processing from the prison guards I was better off keeping to myself. They warned me of possible retaliation since many people doing time feel they were "sold down the river" by public defenders, and the word *lawyer* conjures up the memory. That was only the beginning of the way in which my world became a bizarre downsizing. Guards also told me not to volunteer the fact that I was Jewish. The theory was that inside the skinheads targeted Jews as the cause of all evil.

The shock of entering prison is immediate and demanded my full attention if I wanted to survive. I quickly began to learn what survival required. In prison I witnessed and experienced many of the harsh, unsettling conditions Justice Kennedy noted in a landmark Supreme Court decision, and I came to understand firsthand that in California, prisons are hostile environments with untoward dangers and a culture of distorted, state-sanctioned racist rituals that begin with segregated housing and jobs.

I was moved to write this book when, in May 2011, six and a half years after my release, I read *Brown v. Plata,* the Supreme Court decision that found that California's one-hundred-sixty-thousand-inmate population had been operating at 200 percent over its design capacity for the past eleven years.[2] I was part of that system from October 2003 to November 2005, and I experienced firsthand the dirty, cramped, incendiary conditions. When I read that the court had found California prisons "severely overcrowded, imperiling the safety of both correctional employees and inmates," I began to think about telling my story. Reading *Plata* brought on flashbacks of my experience. Out-of-control, state-sanctioned horrors tend to stay with you, and Justice Kennedy's words kept ringing in my ears: "The California prison medical and mental health systems, sobering overcrowding, and state administrative ignoring of the festering within the system amounts to a broken system beyond repair that results in an unconscionable degree of suffering and death."[3]

Just as people are interested in the notion of prisons, I am interested in peoples' reactions to hearing that I served time in what has come to be known as the California Department of Corrections and Rehabilitation (CDCR).

Respect means a great deal in prison. Although it is an illusory notion, it is one that is constantly in the forefront of every inmate's mind.

In prison I learned how to find a place by learning the rules created by inmates and by learning the language of prison. I conceived this book while serving time in lockups, during lockdowns, and during those times when my physical freedom was confined within the perimeter of a desert prison yard. Reinforced concrete, gun turrets, and rolls of barbed wire contained my movements, but they also stoked my imagination, and I spent the vast majority of my twenty-five months inside recording otherwise mundane events that turned out to be a guide to daily survival.

Before I went to prison, I knew of no one who had been. When I took a half-day tour of Alcatraz on a vacation in San Francisco, I never dreamed I'd one day be spending time behind bars as a prisoner. I had seen a lot of prison movies. I had a healthy dose of curiosity. The idea that human beings are the only species that punishes its own by taking away freedoms played uneasily in my mind. But before I went to prison, I could find no one who could tell me what to expect, no one to tell me how to survive. I walked inside with my senses on high alert and my eyes opened wide and with a conscious decision to listen well and learn as fast as I could. Ultimately prison was like graduate school, and the degree I earned was my life.

Since leaving I have grappled with the subject of all I learned. I've wondered if anyone with a background similar to mine would be interested in reading about prison as seen from the inside. I have shared some stories with relatives and friends, of course. After watching and listening to their reactions to my stories about the living conditions, the food, the gangs and racism, the bathroom etiquette, and even chores as mundane as washing laundry in a plastic bucket, I felt encouraged to write this book. I did the research contemporaneously with my experience—I kept daily journals and wrote volumes to relatives and friends. When I was released, more than three hundred letters I wrote were returned to me to use as primary resources for this book—and they've proved invaluable in bringing back some of the memories that had begun to fade. And part of my research came from the letters I received from incarcerated men. Since I returned to the streets in November 2005, as this book developed, these men provided me with up-to-date information on the prison experience. They report little change inside beyond the growing tensions and massive overcrowding.

This book is meant to educate, enlighten, engage, and entertain. There is much darkness, and there is some light. A sense of humor was critical to me during my time inside, and that holds true today. Humor allowed me to make some unimaginable experiences less hurtful. But it's important to understand that this is not an antiprison book. I realize some people are not fit to function in our society. I have shared meals with such men and have been housed in close quarters with deviants who made my skin crawl. I have met men who slit a stranger's throat and called it "doing work" to earn their "bones," so they might be accepted into a gang. But there is much wrong with prison, too, and I've tried to be accurate for I am hopeful readers will wonder about what legal scrutiny, if any, there has been brought upon some of the matters I raise about yard life.

I hope the readers will get in touch with the notion that the majority of the men and women in prison and those who have experienced incarceration possess important skills and talents that might allow them to make meaningful contributions to society. I will have fulfilled the basic purpose for writing *Derailed* if readers can take the next step and understand that incarcerated people and ex-offenders desperately need society's attention and uplifting hands if we wish to break the cycle of crime and the warehousing of people.

This book does not address the rights of the victims of crime, and in excluding a direct look at this population, I do not mean to denigrate or otherwise minimize the impact of crime on individuals and society. When I practiced law, I represented victims of horrible sexual abuse crimes in the civil arena. I have seen their pain and their resilience, and their stories and their causes will be the subject of another book, another day.

For now, here's my story. Take from it all you can.

Acknowledgments

Three women are primarily responsible for shepherding me to complete this book.

In 2007, Karen Goldman was the first person to really listen to my prison-experience stories and encourage me to start writing. She insisted I record my memoirs on a small dictation machine; I recorded my first session in an omelet restaurant in Scottsdale, Arizona. A resident of Sedona, Arizona, Karen is a three-time published author of books about angels (Simon & Schuster). She guided me to see the spiritual connection between my experiences and the feelings of transformation I write about herein. Karen gave me the enduring gift of a spiritual, caring, and loving view of all life.

In 2009, Cathy Small, a childhood friend and professor and graduate coordinator of anthropology at Northern Arizona University (NAU) encouraged me to write a more academic style book. Cathy introduced me to the notion of my having been a "participant observer" as an inmate. She pointed to my description of human behaviors in prison, in particular, ethnic divisions. Cathy is noted for her 2002 study and resultant book, *My Freshman Year*, when she enrolled as a freshman at NAU. She lived in a dorm as a participant observer, taking classes and trying to negotiate freshman life herself while observing fellow students' emotional, social, and academic experiences. She came out of the year with new insights about repairing the rift between social and academic life and with deep empathy for the financial and emotional challenges of students that transformed her teaching.

From September 6, 2011, to date, Sharon Sprecher (Shayna Punim) used her own shepherding style to encourage me to finish this book. She insisted I let my readers know who I am—whom she saw—to put the content of the book into a real and compelling context. She empathically encouraged me to revisit, talk about, and expand my writing to include subjects I had yet to process; the goal was to help me to relieve lingering emotional pain. I could safely cry in front of her. She frequently reminded me, saying, "Are you writing today?" and putting on the most endearing frown when I said that I wasn't. Sharon prevailed, and for that I am very grateful to her.

I acknowledge my sister—Bobbi Siegelbaum—for unwavering support through my difficulties. She organized a defense fund to help pay my attorney fees. I have much gratitude to the family and friends who contributed to the fund.

I met Steve Frankel in 1997 when we both lived in Southern California. Steve is a gifted psychologist and lawyer. He taught me about the world of psychology and how to evaluate emotional damage in adult survivors of childhood sexual abuse in the legal arena. Steve was there in my darkest times, paid me to do legal assistant work when I faced financially desperate times, and gently assured me I would live through it all. He was right.

I have a deeply ingrained appreciation for the support of family and friends who visited me in jail or prison: my parents, Sylvia and Hesh

Roseman; my sister and brother-in-law, Bobbi and Steve Siegelbaum; my sons Jeremy and Daniel Roseman; and friends Gail and Steve Koff, David Steel, Steve Frankel, and Sharon Bear.

The number of people who wrote to me and with whom I exchanged correspondence that was ultimately returned to me for book reference and research are too numerous to list. They are also near and dear to me. You know who you are.

To my family members and friends who encouraged me to engage in a ten-year cathartic process culminating with this book, please accept my gratitude and deep appreciation.

A Special Acknowledgment to Philip Zimbardo, PhD, Creator of the Landmark Stanford Prison Experiment

It's likely that you wouldn't be reading this book if not for the influence of Professor Philip Zimbardo. I started writing about my prison experience ten years ago, but despite my friends' and family's encouragement to finish the project, my mind kept blocking me from finishing chapters. Eventually I stopped for months that turned into years. I could talk about my experiences, but in my mind, these talks were fueled by surges of adrenalin and became disjointed rants. I couldn't eat whenever conversation turned to my experiences. People listened with interest and posed good questions, but during most of these exchanges, I saw the predictable change in facial expressions from curiosity to astonished fear. I read those changes as disinterest. I know now that I was wrong.

While I was doing research for the book and trying to write about how prison transformed me, I came upon the August 1971 Stanford Prison Experiment (SPE) conceived by Dr. Zimbardo. Dr. Zimbardo's famous study focused on the processes involved in the transformation of regular, good people performing evil acts. The Stanford Prison Experiment—conducted in a mock prison setting in the basement of the university's psychology building—added validity to a fundamental question: What makes people go wrong when faced with powerful situational forces?

The lessons published by Dr. Zimbardo even shed light on the psychological dynamics contributing to the horrific abuses of political dissidents in Abu Ghraib in 2003. The notoriety of the SPE was renewed after Dr. Zimbardo testified as an expert witness for an American reservist unqualified to be a guard assigned in Abu Ghraib, a man who transformed from a good person to a person seriously abusing his "situational power." I read all I could about Dr. Zimbardo's work. I watched his lectures. I came to understand that the outcome of the SPE was part disaster and part groundbreaking. The scientific drive of the experiment was to understand more deeply the psychology of imprisonment.

The experiment was scheduled to run for fourteen days. From a group of solicited applicants, paid fifteen dollars per hour, Dr. Zimbardo arbitrarily selected twenty-four male Stanford-area students whom he then chose to be either guards or prisoners. He gave little direction on how the students were to interact, but within two days of the beginning of the experiment, the students playing guards became verbally, physically, and emotionally abusive to those playing prisoners. On the sixth day, Dr. Zimbardo ended the experiment. As supervisor of the "prison" and overseer of another faculty "warden," Dr. Zimbardo heeded the sharp challenge of a Stanford graduate student after she toured the human laboratory and expressed outrage about what was happening. That student, Christina Maslach, wrote about the SPE: "[Dr. Zimbardo] realized what had been gradually happening to him and everyone else in the study: that they had all internalized a set of destructive prison values that distanced them from their own humanitarian values. And at the point, he owned up to his responsibility as creator of this prison and made the decision to call the experiment to a halt."[4]

As I read more about the SPE, Dr. Zimbardo's influence on me grew. Everything else I had read about prison life was written by academics who had never served time and who thereby lacked a full understanding of the impact on people experiencing a demeaning and often mean-spirited value system.

On April 1, 2015, Dr. Zimbardo and I had a Skype conversation. He expressed his support for completing this book, calling it "an important work."[5] I am grateful to Dr. Zimbardo for his many insights and for sparking my own.

Author's Note

I HAVE TRIED TO recreate events, locales, and conversations from my memories of them and my journals. All the names in this book are real with the exception of the inmates and prisoners and the individuals who are identified as Jenna Fields, Morris Teitlebaum, and Sam Brown, all of whose names, identities, and identifying details were changed. Any similarity between these individuals and any real person is strictly coincidental. All of the people identified as inmates and prisoners gave their consent to use their words providing that their real names or their nicknames were not used.

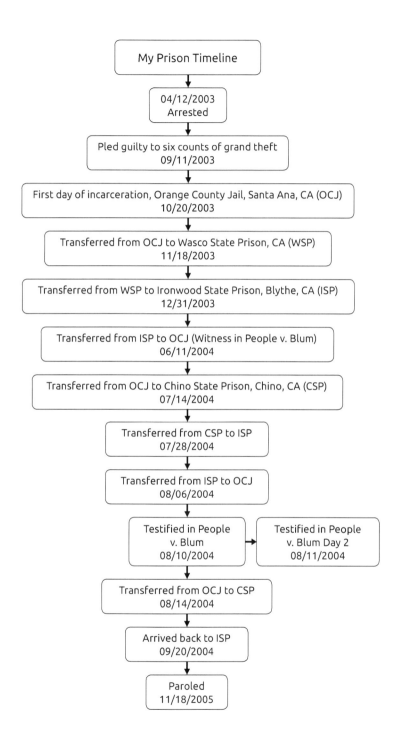

My Road to Prison

Today I made peace with myself and struck a plea bargain in my case. Yesterday there was a full day of testimony by former Blum & Roseman clients/victims. Some people I knew and others I did not. The common thread of evidence was how they were wronged by the conduct of my firm. I sat and listened. I put aside the legal defenses that had been cemented in my brain. Their testimony crumbled the defenses into dusty excuses and I decided to end it and take my share of responsibility.

—E-mail to relatives, friends, and supporters, September 11, 2003

MY SUCCESSFUL TRANSFORMATION, FROM attorney to convict and reentry back to society, took place through closed doors. The journey took guts I never knew I had. The events leading up to the e-mail above—which I wrote while sitting in a dive motel in Santa Ana, California, an hour after my guilty plea to six felonies—hit me hard that day. Still, after a decade of freedom, I continue to rebuild my life, personally, professionally, and financially. This is a story about appearances versus reality.

In the 1990s local media in Orange County, California, gave lots of ink and column space to my wife and law partner, Melanie Blum, and me. Our firm, Blum & Roseman, took on a great many tough legal cases, and the local media featured us as willing legal advocates. Melanie was celebrated when in 1996 she exposed a scandal at a prestigious infertility clinic.

At the same time reporters from magazines, television, radio shows, and newspapers were clamoring for interviews with me because I was representing, writing about, and lecturing about the legal rights of sexually abused children and adult survivors of childhood sexual abuse. I was also noted for my volunteer work as a temporary judge in North and West Orange County (California) courts and for my years of significant service to the county's fee arbitration program. Throughout that decade I heard dozens of disputes between clients and attorneys and decided those disputes, either as an individual arbitrator or as a member of a panel. During the 444-day Iranian crisis, which lasted from November 4, 1979, until January 20, 1981, I served on and chaired the Immigration Law Section of the Orange County Bar Association. Back then, students at University of California, Irvine (UCI) and other venues were easy pickings for not-so-veiled racial profiling. At deportation hearings, my clients were exonerated because they were legal F-1 students. The government prosecutors' contempt for my clients was palpable, and the goal seemed to be guilt by association of legal immigrants, a desire to punish them because of their heritage. The punishment turned out to be living in holding cells, humiliation and shame, the expense of hiring attorneys, and missing a lot of work at UCI.

The *Los Angeles Times* reported on the brave survivors I represented in the 1990s in suits against the Dioceses of Orange and Los Angeles. In those days religious institutions pushed back hard, and without an ounce of compassion, against allegations of abuse alleged against its clergy. Back then, in the face of my client's descriptive testimony during his deposition about having been anally raped with an Easter candle by a Catholic priest, one attorney representing the Diocese of Los Angeles, in a mocking tone, labeled my client as a "fallen out Catholic" and "liar." I learned about this incident in a press conference in 1981 after a case settled with the Los Angeles Diocese. Back then, it was approaching heresy, even for a Jew like myself, to report anything that countered the diocese, its defense, and its brutal Catholic defense attorneys. Not surprisingly, this story never made it to press.

But the media was also in those years closely following Melanie's pursuit of doctors at the UCI infertility clinic, in Orange, California.[1] In 1995, she was beginning to prove that eggs from unsuspecting patients had been stolen and were unaccounted for in the clinic's inventory of frozen fertilized and unfertilized eggs. With her MBA/accounting background, her sharp intellect, and the aid of whistle-blowing employees at UCI, Melanie obtained and digested massive databases of information that showed some unaccounted-for eggs had been implanted in other women with "weaker eggs," while others were rendered useless by being misappropriated to research labs and used in experiments. In other words, both Melanie and I were being hailed as protectors and advocates. As I said, this story is about appearances versus reality.

While this was happening, unbeknownst to me, I was beginning to walk the slow road to prison. That walk began on Saturday, July 19, 1997. The day began great—a day for celebration. The front page story of the Orange County section of the *Los Angeles Times* ran with the headline "50 Couples to Get $10 Million to End UCI Fertility Clinic Suits," hailing Melanie and Larry Eisenberg, the lead lawyers on the case.[2] I had no idea the story would signify the tip of a treacherous iceberg that would eventually sink my marriage to Melanie and our law partnership and drive both me and the firm into bankruptcy. It would also land Melanie and me in prison.

As I read the article reporting the settlement between UCI and the couples—the outcome of a case that began when women who had gone to the clinic for help conceiving alleged their eggs had been stolen—I was unaware of the iceberg. The article quoted Melanie as saying, "The damage is unbelievable . . . at least 15 births had resulted from the misappropriation of eggs alleged in the 50 malpractice suits. These children were robbed of their heritage. The parents were robbed of their children."[3]

Melanie represented only a few of the fifty couples and never did tell me what her attorney's fees from the settlement were. At the start of our law firm, we had established that Melanie would perform and oversee all financial matters related to the firm. While working on her master of business administration and juris doctor degrees, she had been a seasoned forensic accountant for a large furniture store in Los Angeles. Although most people assumed we were rich, we weren't. While our friends were calling to congratulate Melanie on the settlement, our clients' calls increased in frequency; those calls were pressing Blum & Roseman to pay them what they were owed from their settled cases. The fact is, though, we were struggling to do just that. Just fifteen months earlier I had called my retired parents requesting a business loan. When my father asked questions about the firm's financial status, I could tell him only that Melanie handled that part of the practice. Though my

ignorance frustrated me and led me to feel inadequate as I spoke with
my father, I explained: Blum & Roseman had no financial statements. I
could hear the concerned sadness in my father's voice. "Son," he asked,
"how could there be no financial statements?"

Here's the letter from my father dated February 23, 1998.

Dear Mark:

Two years ago, March 6, 1996, you called to ask for a business loan. I
know that it wasn't an easy call to make, but you seemed desperate.
We knew you had financial problems and we understood and decided
to help out.

I do feel and hope the situation is much better for you now. If this is
the case, we should set up a monthly schedule to pay back the loan. I
am not asking for payment up front in full, only an understanding as
to how you can repay the business loan.

Believe me when I say that we were very happy . . . we could help out
in time of need.

The figures are such: $86,418.00 = Total Loan
$37,500.00 = Payments made by you
$48,918.00 = Balance due
Let me know what decision we can come to.

Love Dad

I brought the letter to Melanie's attention. I recall her responding that
my father could wait in line with everyone else, that more settlements
were coming, that he should be patient and not worry. I didn't push
back. Over the years of our marriage, our mode of communication had
evolved; we seldom argued. We both had been trained and had become
experienced in lawyer talk deflection—we were like prizefighters who
danced about, avoiding harsh physical blows. Melanie's blend of sarcasm and anger whenever I mentioned money always prompted me to
dance quickly away. Her motto seemed to be "Always have something
on everyone, just in case," and though I wasn't wholly conscious of my
insecurities around her, I had watched the way she harmed others with
her bullet-like lashes; people seldom knew what had hit them when she
went after them. Toward the end of our marriage—though I didn't yet
know that's what this was—I became more and more conscious of not
wanting to be in the crosshairs of her hatred and contempt. She was

particularly caustic whenever anyone questioned her trustworthiness, and I didn't realize until it was too late, that she had targeted me as a dispensable throwaway.

Almost six years after that first article about the UCI settlement, on Sunday, April 27, 2003, Melanie's photo was once again on the front page of the *Los Angeles Times*, Orange County Edition. This time the headline read "Attorneys Accused of Looting Accounts."[4] The article reported that our firm was being charged with looting clients' settlements on cases we had handled. The total claimed was $1.5 million. The article synopsized our polemic positions: Melanie claimed ignorance of any money having been misappropriated. My attorney responded, accurately: "There isn't any question about it—[Blum] had substantial control and knowledge as to what was going on in the office and financial control over the bank account."[5]

For those nearly six years, between July 19, 1997, and April 27, 2003, I lived in a constant battle with both real and imagined fears. Having been until 1997 an up-and-coming trial attorney, I became a man whose life was on an unstoppable crash-and-burn trajectory. During one five-month period—from October 2002 to March 2003—Melanie and I were ordered to attend what turned out to be nineteen preliminary hearing sessions with our counsel. These hearings were for the prosecutor and the defendants to present evidence to a judge to determine whether there was sufficient and probable cause to believe that either Melanie or I had committed a felony.

During those months, I often sat numb, in stunned silence, as I listened to the prosecution's witnesses giving testimony. Among those witnesses were former clients, Blum & Roseman employees, and bank representatives with signed settlement agreements and checks written to clients on Blum & Roseman accounts. As I heard more and more, I became increasingly depressed. Melanie and I sat at the same table, but she didn't acknowledge me, and as time passed and I came to understand all that had happened, I began to truly comprehend the scope of the deception our clients had endured. I also began to feel aligned with them.

As we neared the end of the prosecution's witness testimony, on March 17 and 19, 2003, the prosecutor brought in the People's forensic expert. During those two days that saw for the first time the financial statements of Blum & Roseman in the form of forensic statements that showed evidence of the tampering and comingling of clients' money with money owed to the firm for attorney's fees. I could barely speak as I listened to the expert testify.

On April 27, 2003, a *Los Angeles Times* article accurately summarized the evidence that had been presented at the preliminary hearings: "Each of the defendants blames the other for misspending the clients' money on business and personal expenses, including a bar mitzvah for their son at the Newport Marriott in 2001. . . . The divorce file contains an e-mail fired off by Roseman before the bar mitzvah . . . : 'The truth is you are paying for our son's celebration at the cost of clients' agony that should be eating you up inside. . . . How do you sleep?'"[6]

Our son, Jonathan, was born July 14, 1988. For his first birthday, Melanie ordered a cake with a gigantic model of the Eiffel Tower floating in whipped cream. He was our joy. Melanie and I had planned that her daughter from her first marriage and my sons from mine would merge into a solid family. Jonathan was the only one related by blood to all of us, and he was a beautiful little boy—a California towhead with blue eyes and as sweet as I could have imagined a child. Sadly, he would eventually become a victim of his parents' personal and professional problems.

Jonathan had studied hard for his bar mitzvah. I worked with him and told him stories of my own bar mitzvah in 1962. After my bar mitzvah, I had continued attending Hebrew school. My parents were members of the Westbury, Long Island, Hebrew Congregation's choir under the genius of Cantor Marvin Savitt. Throughout my childhood, through my senior year in high school, I attended Friday night services with my parents almost every week. As a result, I was able to help Jonathan learn to read Hebrew and to teach him to understand the significance of this Jewish rite of passage. Together we worked to develop ideas for his bar mitzvah speech.

There was, however, one problem, and that was timing. The date of his bar mitzvah was July 14, 2001. Three months earlier, on April 20, 2001, the California State Bar published its decision recommending that Melanie's license to practice law be suspended for three years. They put Melanie on three years' strict probation, and she was furious at me.[7] Throughout the planning of the bar mitzvah, she shunned me. I thought she hated me for not taking the full blame for Blum & Roseman's problems so she could continue to practice law and move on. We had divorced by then, and Melanie was behind in spousal support and demanded I pay for my family members to attend the party after the service. I was appalled and furious in return.

My family and I attended Jonathan's bar mitzvah at the synagogue in Tustin, California, but Melanie barred us from attending the gala event at the Newport Beach Marriott. Someone told me that Melanie hired her own security people and armed them with my photo to ensure that I not enter the premises that evening. Since my family was in town from New York, instead we celebrated my niece's birthday in Laguna Beach; she was also born on Bastille Day.

Three months after the bar mitzvah, on October 1, 2001, Melanie entered a plea before the state bar court admitting to the misappropriation of nine UCI fertility clients' funds. Her plea came in the form of a document called Stipulation as to Facts and Conclusions of Law, and was filed with the State Bar Court Hearing Department, Los Angeles, in nine separate cases.[8] The admissions included gross negligence in not maintaining money received on behalf of clients in her practice trust account, commission of acts of moral turpitude involving money, gross negligence in misappropriating clients' funds, and failing to respond to reasonable inquiries of a client.[9]

Time of Relative Calm

The road to prison temporarily slowed down in mid-2002 and during the first nine months of 2003, which I'll refer to as the Time of Relative Calm (TRC). During the TRC most of the disciplinary action against Melanie was percolating through the state bar court. After Melanie and her lawyer signed the October 1, 2001, stipulation, the activity toward building the evidence to support the road to state prison was inevitable. She had admitted acts of conduct that a DA (district attorney) could view as criminal conduct. The stipulation she and her lawyer signed was in accordance with Rule 132 of the *Rules of Procedure of the State Bar of California*.

California is the only US state with independent professional judges who rule on attorney discipline cases. Charges of misconduct against attorneys are investigated by the state bar of California. If the bar decides that an attorney's actions involved probable misconduct, written charges are filed with the state bar court by its Office of Chief Trial Counsel. Then the court issues a Notice of Disciplinary Charges, which looks and reads much like a criminal indictment. The attorney is served with the notice, and the state bar court sets a schedule for receiving opposition briefs from the attorney, or the attorney's lawyer. The state bar then has the opportunity to file briefs in opposition to the attorney's legal brief(s). The state bar court has the power to recommend the California Supreme Court suspend or disbar attorneys found to have committed acts of professional misconduct (moral turpitude) or convicted of serious crimes.

The state bar isn't required to send its findings to the district attorney where an attorney practices, but nothing precludes it from doing so. I believe that during the lull Melanie's clients who participated in the state bar court hearing made complaints to the Orange, California, Police Department. Our firm, Blum & Roseman, did business in that city. At some point the state bar court exchanged information with the Orange Police Department and the Orange County District Attorney, and that convergence paved the way to prison.

During the TRC, I experienced a bright light of renewed mental health with the help and generosity of my friend Frank Jacobs. I met Frank on August 24, 1975, on my first day of law school at Western State University College of Law (WSU). Frank was immediately open and friendly. I welcomed his friendship because I wasn't looking forward to the "paper chase" competition of law school. Also, at 29 years old, I was one of the older entering freshmen, Frank was six years my junior, a University of the Pacific (UOP) prelaw graduate who knew much more about law and legal studies than I as an animal science major knew. Those factors created the opportunity for an ironic twist of fate during my TRC. The day I met Frank, I also met his UOP classmate from the same prelaw program, Mike Nolan. We three became our own study group throughout our three years of law school. WSU was not a powerhouse law school. In 1975 it had neither state nor national accreditation because it was a proprietary school—that is, it existed to make money. However, a degree from WSU provided the opportunity to take the California bar exam and to practice in all the state's courts, the same as any graduate from a top-tier school.

Study habits of law students vary. Some choose to go it alone, being distracted by group study situations. Frank, Mike and I were among those who found enrichment in studying in a small group, debating, listening, and learning. I was particularly good at making outlines of my notes from class lectures; my outlines were used to guide our group studies, and we called them MER outlines. Mike was studious and tenacious. He drove to school in Fullerton from Pasadena, a three-hour round trip. Frank was an excellent student who put up with the details of the MER outlines but often was distracted by things that had nothing to do with law school. Frank always "got it" pretty fast and challenged Mike and me with legal hypotheticals that strengthened our skills of analyzing a legal issue until we had pounded the life out it. That's what lawyers do.

The three of us also studied for the July 1978 bar exam together. Back then, a multistate question section of the exam was given on a national basis. For the essay writing section, participants were to read a fact pattern, analyze the true meaning of the questions posed, and identify the main issues raised in the fact pattern. We were given three essays, and we had to write on two, with fifty-two and a half minutes allotted for each question. The subject matter could be constitutional law, criminal law, contract law, conflict of laws, probate law or a combination of many topics, the latter referred to as racehorse questions. We took the exam at the Disneyland Hotel, surrounded by monitors and dozens of law students who were freaking out, their only goal in life being to pass this exam. When the time to finish the exams was announced, if you didn't stop immediately, a monitor could void out your entire essay session. That meant failure.

When the bar exam results were released just before Thanksgiving, Frank, Mike, and I were elated to learn we had passed. It was a huge day for celebration. Mike ended up practicing law in Pasadena, and Frank and I stayed in Orange County, where Frank went into tax and probate law and I followed other paths. Ten years later, Frank's lack of patience with the practice of law had him looking for other things to do, and he purchased the G-Bar Ranch in Whitesboro, Texas and became a cattle rancher. Talk about personal transformations.

Whitesboro is in Grayson County, Texas, over an hour's drive north of the Dallas/Fort Worth Metroplex and fifteen miles from the Oklahoma border, which is marked by the Red River. The topography is flat, and there is a lot of topography. In late 2002, as the evidence in the criminal case against Melanie and me was mounting, Frank and his gracious wife, Lori, invited me to move out to Whitesboro, a sea of calm that acted as the perfect distraction from the collapse of my life. My Texas TRC was a life support system. I would have to go back to

Orange County for court proceedings, but in Whitesboro I lived with
Ladys (pronounced Laddis) Jacobs, Frank's mother, whom I knew well
from my law school days. She was a great cook and baker, and she and
I became roommates until I moved to a ranch house on the G-Bar.
Ladys was from Alabama and had never lost the soft charm and beauty
of a true southern belle. She had met Frank's father, Col. Dan Jacobs,
when she worked at the commissary of an air force base in Birmingham
during World War II. According to Ladys, Colonel Jacobs went on
to copilot Air Force One for Harry Truman and was the president's
Arabic translator during negotiations with the Lebanese government
after the war. While her husband was on those trips with the president,
Ladys spent time with her friend Bess Truman at the White House,
and I loved listening to her tell me the stories of those days.

When I moved to Grayson County, the Jewish population shot up
100 percent, but I always felt comfortable and welcomed in Texas. I
got to know and respect the people—honest, hardworking people who
didn't need a written contract for transacting business, just a handshake. To cattle people in northern Texas, your handshake or your
word is your bond. Break that bond just once, and you're not going to
be doing business in Texas ever again.

The Jacobses always made me feel like family, and Sunday after
feeding the herd was fed was family day in whitesboro. This meant
going to church and then to dinner (brunch). Frank and Lori belonged
to a Methodist church in Denison. The services were uplifting and spir-
ited. I enjoyed the pastor's sermons and the resulting sense of belong-
ing. Lori sometimes engaged me in comparative religion conversations
at dinner. She sincerely wanted to know more about the Jewish religion
and traditions. At the same time, our talks were teaching me more
about her devout beliefs in Jesus Christ and his teachings. Later, these
conversations helped me communicate with Christian inmates and
better understand their faith and personal commitments. Knowledge
was important for being accepted into the world of inmates. Many
times these men told me how honored they were to have me in their
midst because Jesus was Jewish, but it was because of my conversations
with Lori that I truly understood the meaning in the context of the Old
and New Testaments.

The other days of the week were workdays. You haven't lived until
you've used a hand hook to physically move three hundred bales of hay

from a flatbed truck into a barn in ninety-eight-degree heat—with 98 percent humidity. At the end of those days, your best friends are a good meal, a shower, and a bed, not necessarily in that order. I learned a lot about agriculture and raising cattle from working with Frank. While I had an undergraduate degree in agriculture with a major in animal science, I knew nothing about the hands-on work of either, much like being able to pass the bar but knowing nothing about the real practice of law.

Frank still raises herds of Charolais cattle. This beautiful white breed of large-bodied beef cattle has its origins in the Charolais area in Burgundy, France. Charolais are raised for meat, and on the open range, I learned how different it was to understand the psychology of cattle in a classroom. In the real world, expensive mistakes happen, mistakes I never had any sense of when I was studying animal science. One such incident occurred when a big "momma" cow refused to move to another pasture with the rest of the herd. Running and chasing after the momma proved fruitless and fatiguing. She was faster, more agile, and much stronger than both of us put together. So Frank and I resorted to using fast-moving vehicles to force Momma to move where we wanted her to go. She still resisted, and the episode only ended when Momma ran herself to death, suffering a heart attack in the field. That was an expensive lesson, but the lunacy and shock of it sent us into paroxysms of laughter.

I was sad when ten months after moving to Whitesboro, in the summer of 2003, I had to say goodbye to return home to prepare for trial. I've not been back to Whitesboro physically, but I do often go back there in my mind. My Texas TRC provided a deep sense of mental comfort during the lonely days of prison I was destined to endure.

That summer, my travels to prison began to move at freeway speed.

CHAPTER TWO

The Back Story

I could feel what was good in me going away, going away perhaps forever, rising after all to the moon, my courage, my wit, ambition and
hope. . . . Nothing noble seemed to remain of me.

—*Norman Mailer,* An American Dream*, quote written in my journal,
August 18, 2005*

N OTHING IN MY LIFE until I was forty-eight years old in
1997 even hinted at the idea that I would end up in prison.
I was born in Brooklyn, New York, in 1949 into a work-
ing-class Jewish family. My sister, Bobbi, was almost four years older.
From the start and to this day, we have been close. Our family moved
to Queens, New York, when I was a baby, and when I turned five,
we moved to Westbury, Long Island, where I attended first grade at
Powell's Lane Elementary School. I was elected captain of the safety
patrol. I'd make sure student patrollers were at their posts assisting
other students to safely cross streets leading to and from the school.

I had lots of friends. I got along well with different groups of kids.
The Westbury School District pulled students from several different
socioeconomic and racial strata in Nassau County. As a result, I learned
to be accepting of all people, never focusing on status or race. I had
always wanted to be a veterinarian, but my poor acumen for chemistry
and math changed my goal to law, a discipline that demanded more of
my natural ability for writing and analysis and my good people skills.

I was always a disciplined child with parents who instilled in me a strong work ethic and the credos "Clean up your room" and "Children should be seen and not heard." My mother did not abide disrespect, and whenever I did show even the least bit of such, she swiftly slapped me across the face. "That hurt me more than it hurt you," she'd wryly say as I burst into tears. I became a rule-oriented child—shy, respectful, and eager to please—a good kid who never got into trouble. At Westbury High School, I was on the swim, debate, and tennis teams. In the mid-1960s, during my junior and senior years in high school, I volunteered scores of Saturdays for the March of Dimes' swim program for special-needs kids. I had a paper route delivering *Newsday* but was too shy to collect my accounts, and my father usually ended up paying money I owed to the newspaper distributor. Looking back, I understand that from the earliest age, I had no sense of the value of my services, and as I grew older, my shyness overshadowed me and turned to passivity. That shyness manifested in a downright fear of girls. Throughout my school years, girls were my friends, good for telling jokes and playing with on the schoolyard, but when adolescence kicked in, my self-confidence vanished. For my bar mitzvah, I invited the most popular girls to join in the celebration, but I found talking to them, much less dancing with them, too difficult. I was comfortable being friends with only those girls who were not popular. I took comfort in their appreciation of my sense of humor.

My father worked in my maternal grandfather's ladies' belt business—Bobbi Belts—named after my sister. My father had been a crew-chief mechanic on war planes in North Africa during World War II, and when he returned home in 1945, my sister had already been born. With a family to support and no time to return to school, he naturally chose to make a living at Bobbi Belts in Manhattan. Each weekday, he took the Long Island Railroad from the Westbury station into Manhattan. Sometimes, on Saturdays, I'd go into work with him to help out; there I used the machines that punched belt-buckle holes or I made points of the end of straight pieces of embossed leather, turning these into usable belts. When the shimmy dress style caught on in the mid-1960s, the demand for ladies belts dried up, and so did Bobbi Belts. In 1966, my parents purchased Leswin Personalized Ceramics, a small business that hired artists to personalize different ceramic design pieces for weddings, bar mitzvahs, and anniversaries.

When I went to college in 1967, my parents moved the business to Avenue S in Brooklyn, not too far from where they had first met as children. Through their hard work, Leswin turned into a major success that eventually led my parents to move to San Diego where my mother still lives.

I met Leslie, my first wife, on October 1, 1967. We both were freshmen at the Ohio State University (OSU) in Columbus, and we met at the on-campus Jewish community center known as Hillel. Although I was still uncomfortable and shy, the familiar environment at Hillel was comforting, and when out of nowhere Leslie walked up to me with her big blue eyes and cute smile, I was able to smile back at her. "Hi," she said, "don't you want to know my name?" I somehow managed to stammer out a response, and she told me she was Leslie. "Don't you want to know my last name?" she asked. Again I stammered but learned she was Leslie Jacoby. "Don't you want to know my phone number?" she asked. In that moment I knew this was the perfect girl for me. She penetrated my shyness and took me by the hand, and after that day, I never dated another girl. Leslie and I quickly became friends, and three years later, before our senior year at OSU, we married.

At Ohio State I was majoring in animal science. Leslie shifted her career choice from preveterinary medicine to education. During the 1968 presidential campaign, she and I worked for the John-Gilligan-for-governor campaign, my entrée into politics that led to a job after graduation in 1971 as a meat inspector for the Ohio Department of Agriculture. There I became only the second Jewish employee of the department. The other Jew was Harry Goldstein, the state veterinarian. Harry made sure I was assigned an inspector job in Columbus. At the time, jobs in Central Ohio were scarce for a guy with a bachelor of science in agriculture who could wallpaper his wall with veterinary school rejection letters. Landing that job was a big deal.

My work as a meat inspector on the slaughterhouse kill floors in Central Ohio was the best education I received—I learned more from those uneducated men than I had from my college professors. The workers called inspectors Doc. "Hey, Doc, we got twenty-seven head this morning—you gonna look the other way on them bad livers?" I didn't look away, but sometimes there were fewer livers to inspect than there were cattle, with no meaningful explanation for that discrepancy. Raw human intelligence coupled with the skill to rapidly wield sharp knives to break live animals into steaks and chops astonished me, and more astonishing still was the sensitivity I saw within the ranks of the butchers and kill-floor workers. I listened to their stories and witnessed the weekend shiners of this drinking, fighting, fucking crowd. I had no idea then, of course, that this would foreshadow my time in prison, no idea that slaughterhouse workers who fought against the grip of alcoholism and drug addiction would be so like the men I would eventually meet in prison. But in those slaughterhouses where I was Doc, workers felt comfortable telling me about their problems with their work, home life, and finances and about their desire to get an education. Many years later, I would experience such confidential conversations in my law office and then later behind walls and barbed-wire fences. I couldn't have known it then, of course, but looking back I see that that experience, along with my law-school training and the experience of practicing law for twenty-one years, honed a natural inclination to listen and cut to the core of a problem in a logical way.

In the slaughterhouses, the other inspectors trained me to do ante-mortem and postmortem inspections. I dressed in a white hard-hat and white uniform with a yellow latex apron down to my shins and industrial-grade rubber boots, and they handed me a scabbard, a knife, a sharpener, and a long-handled hook for grabbing cows' lymph nodes for dissection to rule out diseases. As the only Jew in the ranks of inspectors, I was assigned to work the Columbus kosher kill floor at the Village Packing Company in German Village, a downtown neighborhood in Columbus. At the end of each workday, I returned home to the apartment Leslie and I rented on Chatford Square looking like a mottled canvas of indiscriminate art, splattered with blood on the white surfaces of my work clothes not protected by my yellow apron. I didn't smell too good either.

I quickly built up a tolerance to the things I saw and experienced while working in the slaughterhouses. I saw the fear in the eyes of cattle as they sniffed the smell of death coming from the kill floors. Looking back, I trace my ability to tolerate coping with prison life to these days. On the prison yard, fistfights and bloodlettings with manufactured weapons were frequent. Indeed, one such fight, to my horror, took place right in front of my bunk. In prison, the violence was quick, but I had learned early on to understand that I had seen nothing. In prison, whenever I watched the blood flying, I was transported back to those

Columbus kill floors, and I somehow compartmentalized the sight into a corner of my mind.

Working in those slaughterhouses also taught me that politics is everywhere anyone can make a dollar. I learned that the quality of the food supply is controlled by politics. When John Gilligan, a Democrat, was governor, the state meat-inspection laws were evenly enforced. But things changed in January 1975 when James "Jimmy" Rhodes, a Republican, was reelected to his second nonconsecutive governorship.[1] The owners of a poultry house where I inspected chickens had been strong financial supporters of Rhodes's campaign. The slaughterhouse, an owner told me, was a "Republican Chicken House, an RCH." This meant that if there was a close call about rejecting chickens for human consumption because of a poultry disease called leucosis—a form of leukemia—the call would go to the house. Inspectors were told that leucosis was not transmissible to humans if the yellow, ulcerated skin pustules were thoroughly cooked. Rejected chicken was dyed purple and sent to the rendering plant to become animal food, and this represented a monetary loss to the RCH. Years later, those same lessons I learned in the slaughterhouse, I learned again as a lawyer and then as an inmate: At any given moment, the truth is what people believe, collectively and individually. And politics will run truth off the tracks every time.

Once when I was still a student at Ohio State University, a creative-writing professor asked me why I was enrolled in the agricultural college. "What are you doing with chickens and hogs?" she asked. "You should be in law school!" In 1974, on a Sunday afternoon, her off-hand comment came back to me when I noticed an advertisement in the *Columbus Dispatch* for a law school in Fullerton, California. That afternoon I was still dressed in my bloody clothes and trying to stay warm in the bitter cold Ohio winter weather. Leslie and I had gone to Pasadena while we were still in school to see the 1969 Ohio State versus USC game at the Rose Bowl. As I read, I remembered that January day with the bright-blue Pasadena sky and temperatures hovering near eighty; Leslie and I had both fallen in love with California. Suddenly the idea of applying for law school in California was a no-brainer.

I was accepted, and in the fall of 1975, Leslie and I moved to Anaheim so I could attend Western State University College of Law. She found a position as a reading specialist half an hour away in Chino. Much later, I would transition through the prison there, but in 1975, the prison was definitely not on my radar, and it's only now that I realize how little most people pay attention to prisons or prisoners.

Leslie worked to help put me through school. For three years in law school, I felt as if my brain was in a pressure cooker. To stay on top of the workload and successfully make it to the end, I needed discipline and commitment, but I enjoyed the challenge of learning about things I never knew existed: how the Constitution has evolved to address modern-day legal issues, the elements of specific tortious acts and crimes, how to weave rational thinking together with relevant facts, the need to avoid passionate hyperbole, and the many procedures involved in bringing and maintaining a civil lawsuit for damages. I was mildly interested in criminal-justice courses but saw no relevant application of them to my goals and aspirations at the time.

I graduated in 1978, passed the bar exam a few months later, and was licensed as a practicing attorney in California in December of that year. Like most new lawyers without any real legal experience, when I entered into the practice of law, I felt like a novice skier on a black-diamond slope, one who had lost one ski halfway down. Law school had not provided me the experience I needed to open a law practice, so I learned to fill in the gaps of my inexperience by utilizing skills I'd learned elsewhere. How were lawyers supposed to talk to clients? I improved my listening skills by volunteering weekday evenings at the Anaheim free legal clinic. There I met people with real problems, a striking contrast to the classroom hypotheticals that were the norm in school. I talked to shoplifters, drunk drivers, battered women, prostitutes, and adults who had been sexually abused as children. This latter group came to the clinic because years after the events, they finally felt strong enough emotionally to consider suing the people who had sexually abused them. Working with adult survivors of sexual abuse sparked the legal advocate in me. As I listened to these people and learned about the dark side of their lives, I was jolted out of my insulated middle-class cocoon. In 1979, one year after graduation, I opened my own practice and with a partner ran a small defense firm, Wallin & Roseman. In those years I learned how to be a lawyer.

My partner, Paul Wallin, had a magical knack for managing a law business. Every morning he gave me a complete rundown of the firm's finances. He was a brilliant bookkeeper, able to juggle numbers in his head during his morning shower by using a unique counting method he described as part handclapping and part feet splashing. His brilliant mind was a trap for numbers; not one escaped his mind until it was on a financial statement to be reviewed by our accountant. Paul was also a criminal defense attorney with an uncanny command of the evidence code. He could persuasively argue for the admission of almost any piece of evidence. He was a fierce defense attorney who also knew how to make money. Local press dubbed him the White Knight. Somehow he could persuade jurors to find alleged child molesters not guilty.

Because a guilty verdict does not preclude civil lawsuits, often those men found not guilty in criminal court were still subject to civil lawsuits for damages. These cases alleged assault and battery and, in the extreme, civil wrongful death. The 1995 *O. J. Simpson* case is perhaps the most familiar example; Simpson was acquitted in a double-murder trial but subsequently found liable by a civil-court jury for the wrongful death and battery of his ex-wife. The judgment was $33.5 million.

I was Wallin & Roseman's civil litigation partner. As such, I defended men exonerated by the criminal system. I knew I was defending socially marginalized people. Often during attorney-client interviews, these men disclosed their sexual fantasies; they loved to talk about them, and they kept meticulous records of their favorite child love interests. Because these were confidential communications, I could say nothing about the feelings I had as I listened—their deviant desires were dangerous and frightened me. Later, in prison, I saw convicted child molesters who were kept in constant fear of death by their fellow inmates; child molesters are the lowest of the low on the prisoners' rating scale, even lower than rats.

Because of my conversations with these men, I saw child molestation beyond theory and sensationalized media. My natural inclination was to represent the victims in civil lawsuits as a vehicle for confronting the perpetrators. I knew the process of confronting one's perpetrator could prove a thoroughly cathartic experience for the survivors of such abuse. But it also could revictimize. Over those years I represented dozens of these survivors, men and women. Their emotional fortitude to confront an abuser while at the same time publicly announcing their own sexual abuse ignited my desire to be an advocate. That desire far surpassed my ambition for financial return.

At that time, in the 1970s and early 1980s, those who had endured childhood sexual abuse in California could sue their abusers only until the victims were nineteen. Most of the adult survivors that came to me were older. But because of traumatic amnesia, most adult survivors of childhood sexual abuse don't remember the abuse or aren't able to make the connection between it and the psychological manifestations of that abuse—alcoholism, drug addiction, eating disorders, sexual identity disorders—until years or even decades after they have turned nineteen. Thus, many cases were barred from the courts, and the only way around this statute of limitations was to find a way to change that law.

Between 1993 and 1995, I worked with several other dedicated lawyers to form the Sexual Abuse Litigation Task Force. We became a lobbying organization advocating an extension of the statute of limitations. All task force members worked without compensation, and we paid our own costs to travel to and lodge in Sacramento. After we advocated and testified before the state assembly and senate through an excruciatingly slow and politicized legislative process, the California legislature adopted a new statute of limitations. Adult survivors could now bring lawsuits up to the age of twenty-six.[2] The new statute also provided for civil lawsuits beyond age twenty-six under certain circumstances.[3] This success brought me great satisfaction.

Throughout these years I was still married to Leslie, but over time we became better friends than we were spouses. As students we had much in common, but as we grew older our interests diverged. We had two sons. Jeremy was born in 1981, and Daniel was born in 1985, the same year I was introduced to Melanie Blum. Becoming a father for the first time tapped into a new feeling not talked about in preparenting classes, which focused only on the birth process; my role there was to be the breathing coach. But when my son Jeremy was born at Kaiser in Bellflower, I was present for his birth, and a primitive animal instinct rose up in me—all I wanted to do was protect this bundle of sheer wonderment. I felt similarly when Daniel was born and later with the birth of my third son, but the jolt of that instinct to protect was never as strong as it was when Jeremy came into this world.

At the same time, I was moving away from Leslie. Before I met Melanie, I gave a presentation as chair of the Orange County Immigration Law Section, in Orange, California, and an attorney named Jenna Fields approached me afterward to talk about switching from her legal career in lending law at a major Orange County bank branch to immigration law. I wasn't aware of the true nature of her interest, but my faithful and fearless legal assistant, Sue Lansdon, who attended the meeting and overheard Jenna's complimentary critique of my talk, got it. On the ride back to the office, Sue told me she thought I was vulnerable to this woman's overture for "extra-legal affairs." Her assessment was accurate. Jenna's brilliant legal mind and her interest in me bolstered my self-confidence, and we soon began having an affair.

It was Jenna who introduced me to Melanie. They were friends, both married to doctors and both in the Orange County social fast track that was punctuated by members who were "new money." Jenna told me she thought I could help Melanie locate a new office space in Orange County. In the summer of 1984, the three of us made plans to meet for lunch in Tustin. Jenna and I had yet to talk about her segue into immigration law, but we did continue our romantic involvement. That day as we waited for Melanie, who was more than fashionably late, I realized I was excited about meeting her.

When Melanie finally did walk into the dining room dressed in a fire-engine-red St. John knit that perfectly complimented her gait, her figure, and her blond hair, every head in the dining room turned to look. I watched as she basked in the attention, and I caught myself being mesmerized by the way she moved her head and body. When Melanie held out her hand before sitting, I rose to take it in mine. I caught my breath when I heard her Lauren Bacall–like voice, "Hello, Mark, I'm Melanie Blum; may I sit down?" She always said *Blum* by elongating the *umm* like *hummm*, resulting in Blummm. I was smitten from that moment.

Soon after that day, Jenna and I ended our relationship, though we did remain friends, and she continued her brilliant career in banking and lending law. Very quickly after the breakup, Melanie and I began to meet for lunches that turned into passionate sexual trysts. Both of us felt sexually parched in our marriages, and for some time the love affair with Melanie felt like an oasis.

I recognize that my actions are subject to interpretation and judgment. I include these facts not seeking approval but because they are decisions I made that have a direct link to my road to prison. When Leslie and I divorced in December 1986, I shared the truth with her, and I apologized for all the ways I had hurt her. Leslie accepted my apology and has gone on to become a practicing attorney, remarried to a good man. He has been a good stepfather to our sons.

Within a year of that lunch with Melanie, we decided to form our own law firm. At that time, the law firm of Wallin, Roseman & Klarich was just catching fire. In 1986, little Stevie Klarich—Stephen Klarich—became a partner in the firm. Originally Steve had applied for an open position and I hired him as an associate attorney. I loved this guy immediately. He was a fellow New Yorker, a dyed-in-the-wool Yankees fan, and his eagerness to practice law bellowed out of him with every word he spoke. When I asked if he could do tax-and-estate-planning work, he responded quickly and positively—and I almost believed him. To this day, Steve and I joke about that first interview. He and Paul went on to become premier criminal defense attorneys in Southern California, and since my release from prison in 2005, Steve has helped me obtain documents and answered legal questions.

Melanie, as an outsider to our firm, became the Yoko Ono of Wallin, Roseman & Klarich. I spent a lot of time training Melanie to do trial work. She had not tried a case but had, rather, negotiated settlements in auto-versus-auto cases and had settled some medical malpractice lawsuits. I taught her trial practice by having her sit as my second-chair attorney in a state sexual abuse case and in a federal excessive-force police case. Melanie was a quick study. What she didn't know, she made up.

The defendant's lawyer rose quickly to his feet "Objection: hearsay—double hearsay at that!"[4]

Of course, he was correct. But Melanie, dressed in a St. Johns knit, coquettishly looked up at the judge, who asked, "Counsel, is there any reason why I should not grant this objection?"

"Why, your honor," Melanie answered in that sexy voice thick with bravado, "this question is central to the allegation made in the complaint. This is good hearsay." It appeared that her tactic worked because he said, "Okay, just two questions."

For years afterward, she and I both laughed about that.

In 1989, Paul and I had an angry exchange about the dropping revenues in the immigration side of the practice, and after that argument I left the firm. The immigration side was my direct responsibility, but Paul was right. I reacted defensively. It was time for me to move on, though at the time I couldn't see that clearly. I didn't tell Paul he was right; I simply left. He had been like a brother to me, and I'll always regret the way we parted, a breakup even more difficult than my divorce.

During this time, Melanie and I dismantled our respective marriages and gradually began to cobble together a new family—combining our children on alternate weekends. We married in April 1987. Nine months later, on January 25, 1988, the state bar of California certified Blum & Roseman as a law corporation. We consolidated my Blum & Roseman office in Orange, California, and Melanie's Blum & Roseman office in Newport Beach into a high-rise office building on First Street in Santa Ana. At that time, Melanie was representing former patients against their doctors in medical malpractice cases. Her ability to study a specialty area of medicine and learn the jargon and nuances of the specialty was astonishing. Before going to law school, she had earned a master's degree in business administration and had worked as a forensic accountant. Trained to detect and identify fraud and theft, Melanie then worked for a large furniture company in Los Angeles. Her skills were many and varied. She had taught her mother business accounting for her parents' costume jewelry factory, and she was proud of that. I recall thinking then how right she was to be proud of her skills.

Melanie also helped me feel secure since she had the financial background and training I had never received. When it came to running our firm, Blum & Roseman, Melanie became my Paul Wallin. With her hands-on experience at running businesses and her full command of generally accepted accounting principles to which all businesses must adhere, she seemed the perfect person to do our books. Melanie's becoming the chief financial officer of our small firm seemed only logical. I handled staff meetings, took care of human resources, and coordinated the firm's calendar. It seemed an ideal arrangement at the time, with each of us working in our areas of expertise as well as handling a full load of individual cases.

Writing about Melanie from this distance and perspective is difficult. Knowing her was the most bizarre experience I've ever had, bar none, but reading the legal documents left in the wake of our criminal and divorce lawsuits, I remember more than I wish I did. Beginning in 1999, eleven years after we launched the firm, the procedures and processes of the law slowly became disemboweled; that slaughter is well-documented in the files. I know now that the key to saving everything would have been to work with a concerted defense, selling off our assets to pay our clients and thus minimizing the pain and penalties that loomed in our future. Instead, Melanie turned on me. Under the mounting pressure of criminal prosecution, she began to blame me for everything the district attorney was alleging about us individually and collectively. In retrospect—hindsight is always twenty-twenty—I should have seen much earlier than I did that I was being set up for the unimaginable.

For starters, our discussions about the firm's finances were always short. Melanie's rule number one (and she had many rules) was never to talk about business at home. The operative word was *business*. Business that was good—cases that had just settled or otherwise had good results in court—were exceptions to rule number one. But at home we never talked about any difficulties with office or home finances. Although we were married, Melanie "allowed" me to use an American Express card on her account while she remained the primary account holder. All our finances were controlled by her will. Melanie even issued me a cell phone on her account, and I once drove away from a car lot in a new Jaguar after she told me, with a smile, to just sign here on a deal she had negotiated.

Melanie had a black belt in shopping and could make almost anything happen. She believed in her power, her ability, to finesse the best deal on anything. She successfully negotiated in the contemporary women's clothing department at Neiman Marcus, always refusing to concede. When provoked, Melanie attacked with cutting sarcasm and black humor but never directly to the offender. I'd hear put-downs that included statements like "What does (he or she) know (about anything)? I make more money in an hour than (he or she) makes in a week," and "What does that bitch know about haute couture—did you see the monster thighs on that one?"

I knowingly detached myself from the finances of the firm. One of Melanie's favorite stories—one she often shared with friends and colleagues—was about how I always knew when she had settled a case because I'd come home from work to find workmen's trucks parked in our driveway. Her stories always had a dual purpose: (1) to let me know she had settled a large case, and (2) to lay the foundation for the bragging rights that always came with a large settlement. When people were with us, she spoke as if she had forgotten if those trucks in the driveway were the French-door guys or the carpet guys or the tile guys. I was certain Melanie knew who they were, but she never let on in front of others. After all, she has told me the floor-laying guys were the same men who had laid the wooden floor in the Oval Office. That was her pièce de résistance on the house tours she gave to friends who visited our home, but she was always careful to point out, coquettishly, a home improvement as if it had somehow magically appeared. For example, she might say something like "Oh, right, we put in new French doors . . . I almost forgot."

Sam Brown was Melanie's accountant before she and I met. Once we married and started our firm, he became Blum & Roseman's accountant. The three of us held irregular meetings. Whenever the three of us met for lunch, Sam would threaten to quit if Melanie did not begin to return his calls. The truth was—though I ignored it back then— she usually avoided returning calls when she sensed or anticipated bad news. Sam hated that, but over martinis, she could soothe his fury. Sam and I usually talked obliquely about business matters, but he discussed payroll, payroll taxes, corporate and personal tax returns, bookkeeping, and related financial matters with Melanie alone. That was fine with me. She told me she could handle it, and besides, she was a forensic accountant. I remember her drawling, "Don't worry dahlings," and pointing to the vertical wrinkle I have above my nose. She always referred to it as my *worry line* as she assured me not to worry about finances. "It only makes your worry line deeper." I loved her. I trusted her. And I was happier not worrying about finances since that had never been my strong suit.

Later, at Melanie's trial, Sam testified about his business relationship with me. He told the truth. Melanie, he testified, was the partner he communicated with about the firm's finances. But he also testified that these meetings usually got sidetracked. Sam found Melanie amusing and charming and understood the laissez-faire management relationship between her and me. Remarkably, Sam never produced a financial statement for the firm because he never had enough accurate information from Melanie to prepare one. He remained our accountant until his bills stopped being paid in 2002. That year Corree Riley, our office manager, told me we had a new accountant and Melanie would deal with him on her own. I never questioned the change. Sam had told me he was frustrated by Melanie's evasive answers to important tax questions, the failure of the firm to produce financial information for the preparation of accurate tax returns, and the firm's being three or four months behind on paying his invoices.

At first many of our clients were Melanie's clients, but as a partner in the firm and under the California bar's ethical rules, I also had a fiduciary, or special duty, to protect their interests. Beginning in 1998 and on into 1999, Blum & Roseman clients began to leave calls on my answering machine. They wanted to talk to Melanie. They left several messages. They had been promised calls back. Could I get a message to Melanie to call them back?

Corree was Melanie's right-hand person, and her office was on the same side of the hall between mine and Melanie's. All the firm's financial records were kept in Corree's office. I had no key—another of Melanie's rules. When I needed a check to pay child support, I went to Corree for authorization. Corree's loyalty was first to Melanie, then to the firm, and it was she who knew the bank balances. That was fine with me; I trusted my wife, and when Corree sent Melanie a Mother's Day card, I chalked it up to the closeness between them and never thought twice about it.

Of course, I wasn't thinking that my head-in-the-sand approach toward business and household finances was an attitude that enabled Melanie to raid our clients' money. On August 12, 1999, the state bar of California gave notice of its intent to bring disciplinary charges against her. There were five accusations: charging an illegal fee, two counts of failure to maintain client funds in trust account, and two counts of moral turpitude—misrepresentation. These charges were the foreshadowing of the trouble that would end my career and eventually send both of us to prison.

It was this August 12, 1999, filing by the state bar court of its Notice of Disciplinary Charges that first alerted Melanie to the fact that she was in trouble—but only if she allowed herself to feel others' pain. Looking back, I realize that by April 20, 2001, she and her lawyer knew she had engaged in negligent conduct, when the state bar court found the factual basis for finding her conduct unethical in the handling of three clients' matters. The following is quoted from the court's decision:

Counts One through Three [inappropriate attorney fee agreement, in an infertility case, depletion of funds in trust]

"Respondent's [Melanie's] gross negligence regarding her [attorney trust account] constituted moral turpitude in wilful violation of [legal ethics]. . . . It also resulted in charging the [clients] an illegal fee . . . and in the mishandling of their funds. . . .

Counts Four and Five [medical malpractice case—failure to maintain client's funds in trust] . . .

Respondent's gross negligence constituted moral turpitude in wilful violation of [legal ethics]. It also resulted in the mishandling of [the clients'] funds in wilful violation of [the rules and laws regarding the appropriate management of an attorney trust account]."[5]

These disciplinary allegations foreshadowed others charged against her by the state bar. They all came well after Melanie had kicked me out of the house in November 1999 and when I had no control over business affairs—which was already the established norm.

After subsequent state bar disciplinary charges on September 22, 2000, and January 4, 2001, when Melanie's negotiations broke down, I wasn't aware that criminal charges were coming. Melanie's state bar defense was grounded on making me look as bad as she could and causing me a maximum amount of hardship, including alienating our son from me and the rest of my family. Melanie gave me mixed messages—offering me gifts and playful chatter, complimenting me. Looking back, I see that she was putting me in an on-hold status—in case she needed me. I think her alternative plan was to throw me under the bus, but she wasn't yet sure she would do that.

As I reconstruct the chronology, I see so many clues I chose not to see then. For weeks prior to November 9, when Melanie demanded I leave our house, she had been in a particularly nasty mood. She had begun to withdraw more and more from me in every way, keeping all business and marital conversations to a minimum, coming home late with lame excuses about an elevator malfunction or getting lost while driving. For hours into the night she would stay awake e-mailing, communicating with someone—I had no idea whom. Once I walked into our home office at 1:00 in the morning and found Melanie on the computer, writing an e-mail. When I cleared my voice to speak, she turned and chastised me for sneaking up on her. She blocked the screen with her body and told me to leave. Instead of pushing, instead of demanding to know what was wrong or asking what she was hiding, I simply turned quietly around and walked back to bed.

Then, on November 9, 1999, Melanie and I were sitting across from each other in the family room, separated only by a large coffee table. Jonathan, who was eleven at the time, was asleep upstairs. Out of what felt like nowhere, Melanie looked at me and told me that our marriage was over, that she wanted me to leave and not come back.

I was scheduled to fly to Miami the next morning to present a law and ethics workshop with my colleague and friend Steve Frankel. In what I would come to see as a great irony, our topic for the conference was "presenting emotional distress damages resulting from emotional trauma, in court." That night I packed one suitcase of clothes and sundries, ignoring Melanie's admonishment not to return to the house. The reality that this spelled the end of our marriage would not hit me for a long time. Jonathan was sleeping in his upstairs bedroom, and after I had packed, I walked in, kissed his warm cheek, turned around, and walked back downstairs. I heard Melanie keyboarding in the library and left without saying goodbye.

The next morning I arrived early at Los Angeles International Airport and was sitting quietly in the boarding area when Steve arrived. The first words out of his mouth were, "What the fuck happened? You look like hell!" I smiled weakly at him. I felt like hell, and I felt numb. I told him I had spent the night in a motel by the airport and that Melanie had thrown me out.

Steve's eyes and words said "I'm so sorry."

Melanie never did give me a reason for her decision to kick me out of the house; I only later learned the reasons. When she had insinuated details of her romantic trysts with other men, I had felt as if I were being attacked by torpedoes. The stories she told hurt me. I hired an effective private detective who compiled records of photos and receipts that I never did present to Melanie. I knew, for instance, that her favorite place to meet her married Santa Monica man was off the 405 freeway across from the Long Beach Airport, but I never said a word about it. Later, during the months and years of recovery and healing, memories and lingering feelings associated with those stories revived my internal safety-alarm system. Just as addicts usually have a drug of choice, I was addicted to the idea of being in love with Melanie. I jonesed for her, and because of that I almost always remained off balance, disorientated, and weak. Now, all these years later, recovering from my addiction to love has fueled my drive to regain control over my life. Prison became the laboratory where my determination to do so would be most severely challenged.

Those days at the conference in Miami are a blur. I remember only that Steve and I put on our seminar, but I was walking around in a haze punctuated by panic attacks. The attacks came on without notice. First my heart would increase its pace; I would begin to sweat and gasp for air. Later I would experience this same feeling of claustrophobia in an overcrowded holding cell, but back then the holding cell was the whole world.

I returned from Miami on Monday, November 13, 1999, to discover that Melanie had closed our personal bank accounts; canceled my American Express card, health insurance and cell phone; and told Corree to stop making my child support and car payments. My mental state rapidly declined. I became chronically depressed and came to the realization, right or wrong, that I did not want to practice law anymore. I wanted to run away but had no place to go—until later that place became Whitesboro, Texas.

In January 2000, I began the process of resigning from the state bar. Over the next few weeks, as I struggled to keep from drowning in an emotional black hole, I went to see a few therapists recommended by friends. A psychiatrist put me on different courses of Halcion, Wellbutrin, Prozac, and other psychotropic drugs, none of which I had taken before. They all made me feel like I was piloting a plane that had gone into an uncontrollable nosedive. Many mornings I didn't want to get out of bed, so I didn't.

Four months after that first dark day in November, on March 1, 2000, the California Supreme Court accepted my resignation from the bar. After practicing law for twenty-one years, I resigned with no allegations made against me. By then I had my own apartment in Tustin, equidistant between my sons, Jeremy and Daniel in Irvine and Jonathan in Tustin. Most friends evaporated from my life due to my failure to initiate contact and their inclinations not to favor either Melanie or me. A few real friends from that era remain my best friends to this day. My dearest and most reliable confident was, and remains, my sister, Bobbi.

Sometime in the late 1990s, before the dissolution of our marriage and my resignation, Melanie had retained attorney Arthur (Art) Margolis to handle state bar actions filed against her. The complaints ranged from her entering into unlawful retainer agreements with clients to complaints about the status of money owed clients she represented in the UCI infertility cases. Whenever a client made a complaint, Art was put on notice. He would call the office to talk to me before calling Melanie. In those calls Art asked me to describe Melanie's mood; he wanted to gauge that before bringing news that could trigger her migraines and arouse her volatile outbursts toward him. In those days I was trying to protect Melanie's health and well-being, and I usually told Art to call her back later because most of the time she was nervous as a startled whippet, easily thrown and still more easily enraged.

One day I lost my temper with Melanie in front of the Blum & Roseman staff. It was late 1997, close to the Thanksgiving holiday, and I was in her office, standing in front of her desk. Something she said stoked me—I don't remember what precisely—and I walked out of Melanie's office shouting over my shoulder, "And stuff the turkey up your ass!" I noticed the staff silently cheering, and as those words left my mouth, I felt better, stronger. The visual memory of that moment remains intact, while so many of the specifics of those years blur to blanket sorrow and unease.

Two years after that incident and soon after Melanie threw me out of the house, on Saturday, December 11, 1999, I took and passed the California Department of Real Estate (DRE) exam. That earned me a broker's license so I could start the Roseman Mortgage Company in January 2000. That was also the evening that, out of nowhere, Melanie contacted me and asked me to dinner at Café Piamonte, one of our favorite Italian restaurants. Melanie didn't say why she wanted to get together, but I agreed to meet her at 6:30 that evening. It turned out that she had heard that I had filed an application with the California Supreme Court, a necessary requirement in California, to voluntarily resign from the state bar. The supreme court will not grant resignation to a lawyer if any disciplinary charges or actions are pending against him or her.

As we sat down at the table, I noticed Melanie was dressed to kill. She used her sexiest voice and affection, opened her Bette Davis eyes and looked into mine, and said, "So, I hear you're starting a mortgage company—let's toast to your success." Our glasses kissed. "So, I also hear that you've filed a petition to resign from the bar." I confirmed what she'd learned. Then, in the same casual manner, she suggested that if I took full responsibility for her bar issues, essentially agreeing with her version, I couldn't be disbarred because I'd already resigned.

I don't remember what I said to her, but I know I felt uneasy in my gut and in my head. Something was wrong with this offer. I had drifted so far from the reality that she and I were engaged in battle and that she wanted to destroy me to save herself that I couldn't quite understand my uneasiness. My journal entry from that night reads

> I am to take it from state bar if DRE license not jeopardized— Interesting posturing that is okay and practical—if I am convinced no neg. ramification to DRE license. She sees the big picture I have seen for months—I sense her desperation. JDR [Jonathan] over for the night—organized my frig and shelves—good kid.

Two months after my resignation from the bar, in May 2000, I met in Los Angeles with Melanie, Art, and my attorney, Nancy Hickman. Nancy practiced before the California Department of Real Estate on behalf of its licensed agents and brokers. At that meeting, Art and Melanie asked me to fall on the sword, à la my earlier conversation with Melanie. They asked me to take full responsibility for the misappropriation of money at Blum & Roseman.

To my lawyer's astonishment, I was still weighing that possibility. After all, I reasoned, I had already given up my license to practice law. Why not just take the rap since the state bar no longer had jurisdiction over me? But before I could respond, Nancy declared a break and asked me to meet her in the hallway.

"You're not thinking about doing this are you, Mark?" Her eyes were incredulous as she scanned my face, looking for some sign from me. I could not speak. I stared at her, trying to absorb her words and the reality of what I had been asked to do, and in that moment I began to understand that Melanie's only goal was to save herself. But while making an immediate decision not to go along with the offer I didn't factor in that Melanie would shift everything the district attorney alleged against us in his criminal complaint to me.

A line from Edith Wharton's *The Age of Innocence* best describes that moment in my marriage to Melanie: "he was once more conscious of the values, and of the need of thinking himself into conditions incredibly different from any he knew."

When we walked back into the meeting, Melanie and Art sat up in their seats, hands folded on the top of the desk. Nancy told them I would not accede to their scheme—that it was a half-baked plan that potentially prejudiced me more than it did Melanie—and the meeting ended. Melanie had driven me from Orange County to the meeting in Los Angeles, and on the fifty-minute drive back not a word passed between us. Her anger was projected into her right foot and onto the accelerator of her XJS Jaguar. When we whizzed by the Disneyland exit in Anaheim, I had visions of being on Mr. Toad's Wild Ride.

CHAPTER THREE

The Unraveling

I long for peace and quiet. I have had enough disappointment and hurt
for a lifetime. I have great unknowns. I am an easy target for mean
words and acts—I don't want to reel from the blows anymore. . . . I
feel ready to explode. I don't want to go. Can I make it?

—*Journal entry, June 26, 2000*

I N RETROSPECT, I SEE one day, June 23, 2000, as the turning
point in our inevitable slide that led to prison. That day, seven
months after Melanie had kicked me out of the house and one
month after I refused to fall on the sword, Melanie signed a legal document that had been approved and signed by her lawyer. The document was called a Stipulation as to Facts and Conclusions of Law. In
the stipulation, Melanie admitted to instances of gross negligence for
charging a client an illegal fee and to gross negligence in the handling
of clients' account funds.[1] The stipulation contained information about
me that the state bar court adopted as true, even though I was not
a party or a witness to the state bar hearings, and I had absolutely
no voice in the accuracy of what the records came to reflect.[2] The
California State Bar had made these charges against Melanie almost
one year earlier, on August 12, 1999, but now, by signing the June 2000,
stipulation, Melanie admitted the following under oath:[3] "I plead nolo
contendere to the charges set forth in this stipulation and I completely
understand that my plea shall be considered the same as an admission
of culpability."[4]

Melanie's factual admission reflected the way the firm's trust account, under her control, had not been treated as clients' money but rather as a trough of funds from which our professional and personal financial needs were siphoned. One of the charges to which Melanie admitted follows:

> On or about July 31, 1995, Judith Quinonez, and her husband, Richard Quinonez, retained Respondent [Melanie Blum] to represent them in a pending medical malpractice action in Orange County Superior Court entitled *Quinonez, et al. v. Fulton*, Case No. 746310). In September 1996, the Quinonez case settled for $75,000. The $75,000 settlement draft was deposited in the firm's trust account. After subtracting costs and attorneys' fees from the settlement, the Quinonez's were owed $44,531.27.[5]

> During the period from deposit of the settlement money on September 20, 1996, until the disbursement was negotiated in March 1997, the firm was required to ensure that at least $44,531.27 remained in the trust account. However, on September 27, 1996, the trust account balance fell to $36,880. On October 17, 1996, the balance dipped to $2,102.00. On October 25, 1996, the balance was still only $3554.06. Thus, approximately $42,429.27 was not maintained in the trust account.[6]

I learned of these claims and Melanie's admission only after I requested public-records documents from the state bar in late 2002. This was the first time I had seen Melanie's written admission of wrongdoing. Prior to that, Melanie never admitted to having done anything wrong in either our business or our personal life. Of course she acknowledged making minor mistakes, here and there and now and then, but her wit and verbal powers of persuasion almost always deflected anything negative she might have done. Because we were separated, she and I never discussed the state bar's actions against her, and thus I had no warning of what was coming.

The state bar suspended Melanie's license to practice law for three years, but Melanie appealed her suspension, asking for a new trial on the grounds that I had been the person in charge of the law practice. She claimed that I had control over her life and that more negative evidence was needed about me and her "childhood history of abuse by her mother and father, as well as the history of ongoing abuse by her older brother." Her petition included affidavits by "experts" who had never met me, her parents, or her brother, and had never asked any of us a single question as collateral witnesses. Their affidavits attested to facts based solely on Melanie's claims. Surprisingly, and alarmingly, the state bar court considered the experts' conclusions credible evidence.

In June 2001, the state bar denied Melanie's motion for a new trial. Her motion had included the position that I had used "undue influence in causing her to sign the June 2000, Stipulation as to Facts and Conclusions of Law"—including her admission of gross negligence in handling clients' account funds. Nearly an entire year after she signed the stipulation (and five months after testifying and personally agreeing to the stipulation at the discipline hearing), and after the state bar court announced its decision to deny her motion, Melanie continued to try to repudiate the stipulation she and her attorney had signed. In Yiddish that's called *chutzpa*.

Melanie and I had never talked about these state bar matters, or the stipulation she signed, and the state bar responded to these "new facts in support of a new trial" with incredulousness warranted by the legal circus Melanie and her attorney had created. On November 30, 2001, Melanie filed an opening brief in a request to review and "to repudiate or, at least, ignore the Stipulation."[7] The state bar prosecutor noted the following:

> It appears that Respondent [Melanie] has waited until she got an unsatisfactory result, i.e., the recommendation of a nine month actual suspension, to call foul regarding the execution of the stipulation.[8]

> Here, Respondent [Melanie] had counsel, and is an attorney herself. Testimony at the discipline hearing was that she was a good attorney, and her character witnesses spoke highly of her legal ability. The terms of the stipulation were negotiated at arms' length and took many drafts to hammer out. Yet incredibly she states in her supporting declaration that she did not read the stipulation carefully or understand it![9] [Emphasis in the original]

As all this was going on without my knowledge, I was struggling to regain my footing personally and financially. With my California real estate broker license and a loan from my parents, in early 2001 I founded the Roseman Mortgage Company in Santa Ana, California. My landlord was Jim Riordan, the first client I had ever represented in a jury trial, and in 1997, Jim became the publisher of a book I coauthored,

You the Jury.[10] Despite this firm foundation, after just seven months my business failed. I then became a substitute teacher in several Orange County school districts. I enjoyed most of my classroom assignments, especially in the elementary grades where the kids actually listened to what I was saying. I particularly enjoyed working with the third and fourth graders; teaching the higher grades felt like doing time—no one cared if I was there, and frequently teachers had not left up-to-date lesson plans.

I always introduced myself to the class and wrote my name on the board—"Mr. Roseman"—in large print. Watching fourth graders learn and make associations leading to learning fascinated me, and one day during recess, the level of energy suddenly began to rise exponentially. I could feel the excitement all around and one fourth grader, a little girl, came running up to me. She had just completed three hand-over-hand monkey walks on the bars and was effervescent with joy as she sought my attention. "Mr. Flowerman! Will you come watch me on the monkey bars?" she sweetly pleaded. It's one of my fondest memories of those days.

Meanwhile, Melanie was in private practice. On January 4, 2001, the state bar of California filed 21 new allegations against her on charges that included failure to pay client funds promptly, failure to maintain client funds in trust accounts, and misrepresentation. These allegations became known as "Blum II," and revealed an astonishing fact:

> On or about February 8, 2000, Respondent [Melanie Blum] withdrew the sum of $125,800 from the B&R Client Trust Account and deposited the sum in a new trust account in the name of "Law Office of Melanie R. Blum" at Bank of America, no. 16642-02816.[11]

That money, money Melanie used to start her firm, money taken from the defunct Blum & Roseman trust account, had been meant to be used to pay off our clients. But it wasn't. And so, on March 27, 2003, two years after I assumed that money had been paid, the Orange Police Department investigated Blum & Roseman, and the Orange County District Attorney filed felony charges against us. Again, I had no idea that Melanie had signed another Stipulation as to Facts and Conclusions of Law on October 1, 2001.[12] This time she admitted to nineteen of twenty-one incidents of the same deceptive practices as noted in the

June 2000, stipulation. These two stipulations would later become the foundation for the criminal actions brought against both of us.

That year, 2001, as I was struggling to find my footing personally and professionally, the dissolution-of-marriage proceedings were meandering through the court system. I petitioned the court for an award of spousal support since Melanie was continuing to practice law while I no longer had a license. The court awarded me $1,500 per month in support. Melanie made three payments. On November 30, 2001, Melanie and I entered into a new, nonmodifiable spousal support agreement that had her paying me $40,000, "at the rate of $10,000 on March 1, 2002, $10,000 on June 1, 2002, $10,000 on September 1, 2001, and $10,000 on December 1, 2002."[13] I never received any money from Melanie as pertains to this signed agreement and court order.

After Melanie signed that agreement, I learned from my bankruptcy attorney that she had filed for personal bankruptcy. My attorney subpoenaed copies of her schedules to use to petition the federal bankruptcy court for relief from debt. On the schedule she listed the obligation to pay me as agreed to in November as having been paid in full, but she had never paid one penny of that agreement. When I learned that Melanie and her attorney were to appear for the first time before the trustee in bankruptcy court in the federal courthouse in Santa Ana, California, I decided to attend the hearing as a contesting creditor. When her case was called to review the schedules her lawyer had filed, I could see that both Melanie and her lawyer were visibly disturbed by my presence in the courtroom. Naturally they knew why I was there, since I had previously phoned her attorney to protest the fraudulent statement in her filing. In that phone call, her lawyer was dismissive, but in the courtroom, aware that I was prepared to expose her fraud, Melanie and her lawyer did the only thing they could do under the circumstances. To the surprise of the trustee and all in attendance, they dismissed the bankruptcy petition.

The Orange Police Department (in Orange, California, where Blum & Roseman had its offices) eventually got notice of the complaints about Melanie's state bar actions and initiated an investigation of Blum & Roseman, and Melanie's new law firm—the Law Office of Melanie R. Blum. Depending on the findings of the police investigation, a determination would be made as to whether to take the case to the

Office of the District Attorney, which would review it to determine whether to bring criminal charges.

Melanie had started her firm in Tustin in November 1999. On January 4, 2001, the state bar of California filed its Notice of Disciplinary Charges against her with twenty-one additional counts. On October 1, 2001, Melanie signed a stipulation agreeing to all the allegations (except for two that were dismissed). As discussed, the stipulation included her admission to withdrawing $125,800 from the Blum & Roseman trust account and depositing the sum in a new trust account in the name of "Law Office of Melanie R. Blum" at Bank of America. Had Melanie paid that money to our clients as she had promised, I wouldn't have gone to prison. But I wouldn't know that for another five years, not until 2006 as I prepared to write this book and reviewed all the notes and legal documents. By the time of this discovery, I had processed a lot of information in my head about Melanie Blum. I'd already concluded that she lacked the sensitivity toward others she professed to have and, in reality, was unable to find fault in herself, always looking to hang anyone who got in her way. I was a survivor of her hatred, and discovering she had transferred our money and our clients' money paled in comparison to all the hurt and humiliation she brought upon me. Still, she did not destroy me.

On March 27, 2002, when the Orange County district attorney's office filed charges against us, my sister, Bobbi, started a defense fund for me, and I hired a well-known and respected Orange County defense attorney. Although I tried to talk sense to Melanie—suggesting we put together a concerted defense and sell off what we had to pay off former clients before the district attorney lodged a criminal complaint—she refused to even talk to me.

My lawyer approached hers to suggest our working together to put on a common defense, and again Melanie refused, this time through counsel. At the time I couldn't understand why. Now, having read through all the papers from her state bar case, I understand that by that time she had dug herself in too deep by her accusations against me. So, on April 12, 2002, on what would have been our fifteenth wedding anniversary, we were arraigned in Department C55 of the Orange County Superior Court. I'd been in that department dozens of times before, always representing clients in trouble with the law. Being in that room filled with attorneys and clients milling around, I felt strange suddenly being the defendant. Several attorneys I knew refused to even make eye contact, while others shook my hand and wished me luck. My heart was pounding, and I was flooded with embarrassment as I looked at the clerk checking in counsel for their appearances. I knew her. She asked what case I was on. I nearly choked on the words "my own." Her face registered her shock.

That day we pled not guilty, but by then our legal defenses were polarized. Melanie accused me of being the one who was "in charge of the firm's finances," and claimed she had had no idea that I'd "misappropriated and mismanaged" the firm's money. My lawyer argued that it was Melanie who had had control over Blum & Roseman finances, a true but hollow defense. As a signer on the trust account, the law made me equally culpable. At Melanie's criminal trial, her lawyers would bring evidence that my signature stamp, which I never used, was on the majority of trust checks that had been used to steal clients' money from the firm's trust account. Over time, the case only became more and more ugly and convoluted but the facts were clear from the start. The evidence did not discriminate between Melanie's criminal intent and mine. I was connected to the theft and to the thief and could not legally extricate myself from imminent prosecution and certain penalty.

Of course, at the time I had no idea, but on that day we handed the deputy district attorney a prosecutor's dream: antagonistic defendants. When codefendants point their fingers at each other, the DA knows that they are each on a self-destruct trajectory, that jurors are likely to hate both and to find both criminally responsible. If the business partnership is also laced with domestic spite, there's even more likelihood of this. Our cases had to be bifurcated. We would have to have separate trials.

The only silver lining was that we were out of jail, without bail.

The judge had clear legal authority to divide our cases upon a showing of prejudice to one or both of us. Thus, on June 10, 2003, a Motion to Sever Trials was filed. The motion came three years after Melanie's confession of gross negligence regarding her handling of clients' trust accounts. I had not yet read those files, but my attorney offered this written motion:

> Initially, an "incriminating confession" by the only codefendant Blum, is potentially an integral part of this case. Prior to the filing of the

pending charges, Blum was tried before the California State Bar on the same subject matter involved in the instant case, to wit, the misappropriation of client funds from the Blum & Roseman Client's Trust Account. During the pendency of the state bar disciplinary case, Blum made several incriminating statements or admissions against herself, as well as defendant Roseman. These prejudicial statements serve to incriminate Roseman, her former husband, by not only blaming him directly for the alleged misappropriations, but also claiming his mental and physical abuse caused, excused or mitigated her admitted wrongdoing.[14]

In other words, part of Melanie's throwing-me-under-the-bus plan called for launching as many allegations against me as possible. Her charges ranged from spousal abuse (which a jury rejected after a so-called expert she flew in from Florida, a woman who had never met me, testified I was abusive) to her accusation that I had forced her to have an abortion (no one ever forced Melanie to do anything), and when she got pregnant in 2002, she made the decision to terminate the pregnancy *sua sponte*—on her own. "Are you coming with me to see my OB, or am I doing this alone?" she had angrily shot at me at the time. And so I went with her when she got her abortion; I wish I hadn't. While there, I felt as if I were an outsider and Melanie and John, her OB, were on a date—such was the state of their misplaced flirtation.

Her manipulation of our son in an effort to have him testify that I had been sexually inappropriate with him was Melanie's crowning act of evil. She did this while I was living alone in an apartment in Tustin, after the state bar court had ruled against her. The Tustin Police Department began to investigate Melanie's alleged charges of abuse. Investigators questioned me and told me that the case would likely be refused by the prosecutor for lack of any evidence and because of my son's inability to provide specific details about what his mother told investigators I had done. Ultimately the trial judge refused to allow Jonathan to testify for lack of any factual basis to Melanie's accusations.

But Melanie and her defense team did not stop there. I was their bull's eye for all their bull, and all of Melanie's accusations were bull. In other court documents, Melanie made sexual-abuse allegations against her father and older brother. I do believe her father had been abusive to her, whether sexual or not I'll never know for certain. I do know her older brother French-kissed her in greeting at all our family get-togethers. Melanie walked the fine line between being incapacitated and unable to function under pressure of work and trying to convince the state bar that she was sufficiently competent to practice law.

In relation to me, Melanie's criminal defense circled around three themes: first: her physical health and her mental state; second: because of that first defense, that I had taken over full control of the firm's finances; and third: because of the first and second defenses, and because she was overworked and distracted by her involvement in the UCI infertility cases, that Melanie had had no idea what was going on with our professional or personal finances.

These three themes emerged in an April 20, 2001, decision by the state bar court, Los Angeles.[15] That decision recommended suspension of Melanie's license for three years, but the court stayed the suspension in exchange for three years' probation based on its reliance on the testimony of a psychiatrist, Dr. Sharma. Dr. Sharma, whom Melanie had retained, devoted 90 percent of his time in his professional career as a forensic expert in court.[16] He had testified in state bar cases a hundred times. According to Dr. Sharma's report, he had spent about one and a half hours talking to Melanie.[17] He and I never met. Although as a lawyer I'd become aware that plenty of experts will testify against anything, including motherhood and apple pie, I was stunned by Sharma's gall. Melanie and the state bar had paid him to figure out what contributed to her problems between 1995 and 1997, the period of time she had admitted to having charged an unlawful fee and having misappropriated clients' money. The court's opinion stated, in part, the following:

> Dr. Sharma acknowledged that respondent [Melanie] was heavily involved in the UCI fertility cases which required that she spend long hours focused on related legal problems rather than focusing on how her husband was running the law office at the time. [Melanie] was under stress because of the complexity of the legal issues and the number of cases involved. She took on too much work. This impaired her ability to cope in financial matters involving her clients being handled by Roseman at the time. Her symptoms included anxiety, short temperedness and disorganization, including not keeping tabs on the client trust account.[18]

To my astonishment, the state bar court continued to find the psychiatrist's report worthy of factual reliability:

Moreover, Roseman was a verbally-abusive husband, who often raised his voice to her, threw objects at her and made it clear to her that he would run things at the office and that she had to focus on the UCI cases which promised financial rewards for the both of them. Respondent described Roseman as a pathological liar—a person who lies even where there is no reason to lie.[19]

Dr. Sharma is also quoted by the state bar court as reporting that during their one-and-a-half-hour interview, "She was all over the place during her evaluation. She was receiving calls on her cell phone relating to pain medication being prescribed for her by Dr. Susan Powers."[20]

The expert went on with testimony relied upon by the state bar in its decision, that "Dr. Sharma believed [Melanie] was truthful in recounting the circumstances of 1995–1997." In Dr. Sharma's opinion, these events would cause the misconduct to which Melanie had agreed as factual.

Melanie also brought in her board-certified treating psychiatrist and UCI faculty member, Dr. Sporty, for his opinions concerning the gross negligence plea of his client. Again, here is a quote from the state bar court's decision:

> After an unsuccessful attempt at saving the marriage, [Melanie] continued in therapy with Dr. Sporty and continues to see him twice a week.
>
> Dr. Sporty's initial diagnosis was post-traumatic stress disorder. He found [Melanie] to be extremely anxious, depressed, confused, and prescribed various medications that she rejected because of side-effects. She was also taking medications for migraines. He described [Melanie]) as a person in "crisis."
>
> Dr. Sporty found a connection between [Melanie's] abusive, dysfunctional marriage and childhood verbal abuse by her mother, physical and verbal abuse by her older brother, feeling unsupported by her mother and her strong belief that other persons would not believe her if she complained.[21]

On October 1, 2001, two years after I had stopped practicing law, Melanie again pled, at the state bar court, to conduct involving nine cases of misappropriated UCI fertility clients' funds.[22] In exactly two years to the month, I would be serving time in prison for many of the charges for which Melanie took full responsibility that day. Three years later, on October 17, 2004, Melanie was convicted on ten of twelve felony charges against her. On that date, she was placed on interim suspension by the state bar of California. This meant she was not eligible to practice law. Six months later, on April 14, 2005, the state bar filed a motion in the Orange County Superior Court to allow its representatives to shut down the Law Office of Melanie Blum based on information "that professional and unlawful misconduct continues to occur at Blum's law office." Based on a tip from the public and after confirming that the website for Melanie's office did not provide notice to the public that she was unauthorized to practice law, the state bar had set up a sting operation. State bar investigators called Melanie's office for a pretext legal problem involving reproductive law and made appointments to see her for legal advice. The judge hearing the state bar's motion granted it and ordered Melanie's practice shut down immediately.

In essence, this was my road to prison. I do not hope to reindict anyone by going over the facts and collecting and comprehending the public record. At the time, there was much I didn't know and didn't understand. This macabre adventure taught me important lessons about myself and about the world around me. Most importantly, it opened my eyes to how I can make better choices in life—particularly why I must choose to respect myself.

CHAPTER FOUR

First Rodeo

I know not whether Laws be right,
Or whether Laws be wrong;
All that we know who lie in gaol [jail]
Is that the wall is strong;
And that each day is like a year,
A year whose days are long.

—Oscar Wilde, 1898

IF IT'S YOUR FIRST prison term, it's your *first rodeo*, a term I learned on day one in county jail. As a kid I had seen Roy Rogers's rodeo at Madison Square Garden, so the term had an entirely different meaning to me that first day. Like all new arrivals, I'm sure my face registered the shock I felt, though I tried to look deadpan. Along with the shock came the immediate need to run—anywhere! I wanted to sprint and get out, but I found nowhere to run. Few know how to deal with the shock of jail or prison unless they've already experienced it and it's imperative to learn fast. One good way to get educated is from a seasoned inmate, or OG, original gangster.

OGs are unruffled, and they proffer time-seasoned wisdom. I first heard that term in Orange County Jail (OCJ), before I was processed into the county jail system, and later when I "caught the chain" to state prison. We were awaiting bunk assignments in a crowded holding cell for eleven hours. During the time, without a lull, the thirty-by-twenty-foot cement cell reverberated with loud voices, shouting, singing, preaching, and complaining. There was no weeping or whining, just a lot of depressed faces. An OG naturally picked me out of the crowd as a "fresh fish."

The OG was sitting on a cement bench that ran along the perimeter of the wall. He was observantly watching, occasionally talking, never shouting, just "chillin'," as he would put it. He projected calm within the storm. He was in his late 60s, Mexican, with dark leather-like skin and steely black eyes. He exuded the confidence of a man who had experienced many rodeos, someone for whom there were no unknowns about the system. Because he seemed comfortable and nonchalant despite the madness and fury all around us in that holding cell, I wanted to talk to him. I waited for a place on either side of him to open up so I could sit beside him. After what felt like hours, a guy beside him stood, and I moved into the spot. I didn't have to say a word. "First rodeo?" he asked. I nodded. Without my having to ask, he said, "Let me tell ya how to get through this—remember two things: (1) be as invisible as a ghost, and (2) do the time; don't let the time do you." The ghost part puzzled me.

"How can I be invisible in overcrowded places?" I asked. He gave me a long, sideways glance and said, "You'll have to figure that out for yourself. No two people experience prison exactly the same way." It wouldn't be long before I learned that being a ghost means blending in with others of your race for protection. It also means helping other inmates with requisite sensitivity and with no expectation of receiving anything in return. A ghost isn't seen as a threat.

Once I got to prison, I quickly realized that compared to the other prisoners, I wrote a lot of letters. As a result, others noticed and began to come to me for help with spelling or to dictate letters to their families and friends. I made no secret that I had been an attorney, and that news telegraphed its way around the yard. Having been an attorney provided me the opportunity to become a ghost—to answer legal questions inmates had and to teach them about immigration, probate, divorce, and related issues about which they had few clues. I helped by drafting letters to lawyers on the outside who were preparing petitions or appeals related to the poor medical care of their clients. As a practicing attorney, I had learned to document events and significant facts, and this I did inside. Like everyone else, most inmates are happy to learn if the teacher makes them feel comfortable and respected for what they already know rather than judgmental about what they do not.

The OG's advice to "do the time and not let the time do you" became my mantra that ran constantly through my mind. When I allowed the feeling of time doing me to reach my consciousness, that is, when I began to feel each second, minute, day, month, and year, a surge of crippling anxiety flooded my mind and body. In those times, the weekends and holidays were especially difficult, slow and weighted with sorrow. That, I came to understand, was what happened when I let time do me.

One night in the first weeks of my incarceration I had a nightmare. I was in the upper bunk in a two-man cell. I was being dragged toward the edge of a floating saucer and pulled over the edge of that saucer by an unbearable force. It felt like the force of the ocean. As I was pulled closer and closer to the edge, my body felt as if it were no longer being pulled; rather, my mind was being yanked over the side. I woke before I lost my mind but only after I had experienced the feeling of being out of my mind. After that, the dreadful sense of time doing me never again returned. I worked to stop my mind from going overboard.

On October 25, 2003, I wrote my first letter to my parents from the Orange County Jail. It's clear to me when I read it now how I was handling those first five days of lockup.

Dear Mom & Dad—

Writing to you from this world feels strange. Part of my mental adjustment techniques have included insulating myself from thoughts about the outside. Writing to you necessarily makes my two worlds collide—but that is just another adjustment I shall have to make. . . . It is intense here—and it is mellow—the conflict in environment is created by design—I know this. . . . I have been yelled at by personnel for shutting a door that didn't need shutting, for following conflicting orders—that was my favorite—and for not pulling my pockets out for inspection after a meal (to ensure I did not take a plastic spoon, or god forbid, food, back to my cell).

Orange County Jail has no windows to the outside, and as a result, once inside, I lost my sense of time. There are no clocks on the walls, and watches are contraband, so my inner clock charted the time of day with pangs of hunger. Time passed without shadows. The sun was gone. Weather was gone. And time was further eclipsed by the confusing architecture—open vestibules, closed corridors, mazes designed to slow inmate movement. All this culminated in my feeling of being lost. I felt like I was in a hole in the ground. My lungs felt tight with a lack of oxygen, and this caused malaise and an everlasting desire to sleep.

Once assigned a cell, like everyone else I was put into a program. The program is the inmate's daily routine and it tells you when to wake, when to eat, when it's time for day room television, when to make phone calls, when count happens, when mail arrives, when it's time for exercise on the caged-in roof, when it's time for medical attention, and when it's time to go to sleep. The program guided my time and created boredom.

To break the monotony, most inmates become creative. *Jack shacks* are one example: designated showers designed for privacy with a worn, crusted, opaque curtain—the inside full of plastic-protected contraband pornography. Enter with your imagination, come out relieved. The jack shack shower was treated as sacred territory.

During a first rodeo, most inmates also meet people they've never even imagined existed. I met a car thief with fifteen aliases, grown men who were illiterate, television junkies whose social skills derived from television talk-show palabra, Jerry Springer and Maury worshippers—men who watched these shows while holding their breath awaiting DNA tests for alleged fathers. Whenever testing vindicated the guy, these men stomped joyfully around the television room in a sort of victory dance, offering ear-piercing screams about "the whore." During a first rodeo, what constitutes comfort in living conditions requires a sharp shift in expectations.

> My living conditions are "charming." I share a cell with 5 other men. The cell is small—about 20' x 15' and has one stainless steel toilet and a sink—all in one—in one corner, without any walls—no privacy at all. I learned to leave my modesty outside, so I do okay. Most of the day we are locked in our cell. One guy has been here for seventeen months. He is top dog—he is very clean and has set a high standard for wiping the seat after peeing.

> I read a lot—anything in English. Mostly mystery novels. They take me to a world outside these walls and that is good. I take naps, brush my teeth—wipe the seat (with strips of newspaper)—that's a typical day.

> —*Letter to my parents from the Orange County Jail, October 27, 2003*

At this early point in time in my term, I had not yet fully experienced the humiliation and shame that is projected onto inmates by the administration, the guards, and other inmates. But that time wasn't long in coming.

Humiliation and Shame

The walls are posted with the rather sobering signs that frighten and humiliate: "Warning, No warning shots will be fired." (Isn't that a warning?)

—*Letter home, October 30, 2003*

After only three weeks in county jail, I was loaded onto a CDCR bus with forty other men and moved 170 miles north to the reception prison in Wasco, California. I was moved into a dorm the size of your average Costco. The first thing I noticed in the dorm where I was housed were the No Warning signs, and these especially bothered me. They were posted on the wall of the cavernous dorm, a reinforced cement "large box" structure—one door in, same door out—with no windows. Columns supported the weight of the roof since the place had no interior walls. At either end of the roofline where the twenty-five-foot-high walls connected with the nine-hundred-foot-long roof, sliding garage-door-like structures opened and closed. Through these doors guards could enter with rifles pointed down on the inmates. Whenever those doors slid open, my heart stopped. Men in black aiming long guns would step out shouting, "Drop to the floor."

Sharpshooters can shoot a toothbrush out of a hand or take down a guy with a threatening knife. I witnessed both these feats from just feet away. The clap of the shot roused everyone to instinctively dive for space under a bunk. Inmates have few safe places, and at the sound of those gunshots, panic sets in fast. I learned the No Warning signs meant that bullets ricochet off cement surfaces (even after penetrating a body), so don't make us shoot. The first time the guards poured through those doors, I was flooded with shame and indignation and the sense of being a fish in a barrel, vulnerable to being shot at because of someone else's stupid act. This feeling became a lasting metaphor of the danger of prison life. It was a lesson well learned.

Shame or humiliation is a feeling of pain that courses through the mind and body when someone looks down on you. It's the feeling experienced by children forced to wear a dunce cap and sit in a corner. It's what people feel when they are forced to offer information against their will. I think of the acts of humiliation and shame in the 2004 Abu Ghraib prison incidents—there American soldiers used degrading tactics to arouse fear and shame. The well-known picture of an Iraqi detainee forced to stand naked and hooded with electrical wires attached to his genitals was humiliation by design, meant to induce shame and maintain control. No one wants to be humiliated, and prison administrators know how to use shame as a tactic. They use it in the name of "safety."

Inmates, however, miss nothing. Inmates are masters of human conduct and emotions who learn to read people as if they were transparent. In my time in prison, I met several polished and intelligent con artists who possessed sales skills exceeding even those of the most skilled real-estate agents, investment advisors, politicians, and trial attorneys. But the mind of a criminal usually is unilateral—by which I mean most criminals think only about what will most benefit them.

Over the years I was inside, I came to know the eerie thinking that drives the criminal mind. Making a living as a criminal requires the ability to let go of any second thoughts about stealing an identity, a car, secured information, or a reputation. The true criminal mind reads weaknesses, often even after only a brief encounter. Seasoned criminals know how to instantaneously read subtle body language and facial expressions. Criminals who plan to steal are able to instantly psychologically evaluate their victims. The focus is on determining, in an instant, whether their target is gullible, easily distracted from details, trusting, empathic, and too humiliated to report having been attacked.

My first cell was far from what I had seen in movies about prison. I was paired with Billy W. in a four-by-ten-foot cell made of reinforced concrete with a two-inch-thick clear Plexiglas bulletproof sliding door. Billy smoked although smoking was against prison rules. I could ask Billy not to smoke, but if I did, I risked humiliating him and that, in turn, made me feel humiliated and stopped me from asking him. Porters—inmates pushing carts filled with reading material—smuggled handmade cigarettes into our cell. To light the smokes, a lit rope crafted from toilet paper and ignited in a wall socket was serpentined down the corridor of cells and under the space between the Plexiglas door and the floor. Next to the lower bunk, in the corner where my head rested, was one freestanding, stainless-steel toilet/sink. Water came from a tap on top of the toilet. The cell was designed for efficient use of space and, I began to realize, the layout was punishing to the ego and self-esteem. Social etiquette regarding bathroom privacy is nonexistent in prison. Everyone is easily observed at all times; partitions play no part in prison architecture.

Before prison, I had never experienced humiliation by design, but there I was, in the midst of a circus of humiliation. The rationale was that shame was part of the punishment, part of inmates' experiences every moment of confinement. Though never openly acknowledged, it is always a motivator for disharmony in the yard. When every message tells you you're unworthy of being part of society, not good enough for anything decent, the mind reacts predictably. One obvious result is the insidiously uncontrolled gangs that dictate so much of the way the California prison system runs. In my experience, prison administrators and their enforcers work to instill feelings of inadequacy, powerlessness, inferiority, stupidity, and being different on all inmates. Those are the tools of prison.

Ironically, in their tribal behaviors, inmates press hard on the same emotional buttons. In prison, mind control and physical control go hand in hand. In just moments, the natural leaders and the natural followers surface. Those who master the ability to make others feel inadequate, stupid, different, powerless, and inferior become leaders, men who have the respect of everyone else on the yard. Making an inmate feel inadequate starts right away by taking away an individual's name. Inmates are never addressed by name.

It was in Wasco, in reception, that I first became number V12214. I spent the whole first morning in reception in brief interviews with administrators and medical people, the system known as classification. I recognized right away that the medical staff did not shine and most administrators were bitter, resentful, and heavy with a sense of their own authority; after all, they were the postconviction deciders. Regarding health issues, the staff followed an intake questionnaire that asked about prescription drugs, history, present conditions, and the location of tattoos, needle marks, scars, and bullet wounds. After those interviews, I received my photo identification card stamped with my CDCR number.

From that moment on, inside I was never Mark Roseman; I was always only V12214.

To the CDCR, I still am V12214. My certificate of discharge issued by the department is a wallet-sized card bearing my name, number, date of discharge, and the statement: "The above-named person has been discharged from the jurisdiction of the California Department of Corrections on all existing felony commitments as of this date." The wording is ominous and foreshadows the fate of far too many prisoners. The total three-year recidivism rate (returns to state prison) for all felons released during fiscal year 2008–09 was 61 percent.[1]

I read the statement this way: "Mark Roseman is an ex-felon, and we're ready for him to return to society, as most discharged inmates do." In other words, the humiliation remains with the implication that this person may just not be good enough. The CDCR number remains forever and is reactivated upon an inmate's return to the system—whether he's convicted of a new crime or sent back for a parole violation. The CDCR number tracks inmates through the system. At any time, a guard or other prison official can demand to see an inmate's photo identification card and hear a rapid recitation of the number, and any mail sent to an inmate that fails to include the CDCR number will likely be either greatly delayed or "lost."

Every question an inmate is asked at orientation reminds him he is different—and not in a good way. All inmates, except those physically disabled, must have a job, and this job is determined at orientation. My job orientation meeting was heavily tainted by the administrators' indifference and curious paranoia about the information contained in my C-File (central file), where the crimes for which I was convicted were briefly summarized. My interviewers expressed fear of my past: "You're a lawyer and must be insulated from influencing the others." When I asked what that meant, the interviewer snapped, "Shut up— this isn't a court of law." I had nothing to say after that. I sat, watched, and felt my life evaporating out of my control, handed over to those who had indelibly classified me, fitting me into a stereotype about which I had no say.

"You're not going to be around any computers," the interviewer told me. Inmates are allowed no contact with computers, with or without Internet capabilities. "And don't think about any inmate unions or filing no crazy lawsuits for the riffraff." One sergeant asked the assistant warden if I could work in the warehouse, to which the assistant warden shook his head. "Too much opportunity to cheat and steal in there," he said. I could not defend myself during this ordeal. Rather, like the others, I was forced to listen to disparaging remarks without being able to respond. After that interview, I was relegated to a porter job. I resigned myself to excel at this job, and so starting that day, five days a week, I cleaned prison toilets and showers. I had wanted to work in the yard library, but the sergeant told me I could do so only as a porter, not a librarian. Eventually I would become the only librarian/porter on the yard, but that's another story.

Humiliation between inmates is also a serious matter, and early on I learned all the ways inmates can and will humiliate each other—and the repercussions of doing so. Calling another inmate out for anything in front of others is called putting that person "on Front Street." When I first heard the term, I was lost, but eventually I learned it meant putting another inmate on the defensive, even if the reason you called him out was 100 percent legitimate. As I came to understand the idea, an image came to me. I imagined us on a movie back lot, a tree-lined Main Street, with a man with a bullhorn shouting, "Limp Dick keeps his radio on too loud at night." The next scene in my head was of inmates holding their palms to their ears yelling, "Pull the plug on that shit."

Humiliation is complicated and relies on enhanced senses to read situations in a flash and to act or react in socially acceptable ways. Over the years, as I was moved from county to state and from institution to institution within the state system, I discovered that every environment of captivity had its own local rules of conduct between the races. One rule remained true, however, in every institution: blacks could not use the same toilet as whites and gang (multiple person) showers were segregated by race. Inmate rules, sanctioned by the prison administrators, regarding segregated eating, separate sports activities, and restricted exercise yards, have their origins in humiliation rituals learned on the streets.

Being told what toilet bowls the whites use and where the other races must move their bowels is degrading enough, but to maintain the continuum of segregation, dominance, and power of the whites, behind that humiliation is the real message: follow the rules and don't try to change anything. Prison exaggerates emotions. Each day becomes more and more grating as the internal tug for freedom waxes and wanes in that part of the inmate that is always free.

If there were a Ten Commandments for prison conduct, "Don't put anyone on Front Street" would be among the top three. It's big. Think about what you've heard about the infestation of prisons (and towns and cities) by gangs. As time passed, I thought more and more of the commandment I'd learned from that seasoned OG back in the Orange County Jail: "Be like a ghost. Don't be seen and don't say nothing; don't look nobody straight in the eye." Staring at anyone ever so briefly can trigger confrontation: "You mad doggin' me, muthafuckaah?"

One day into my journey through the system, just after I'd arrived at Ironwood State Prison outside of Blythe in the hot, empty desert, I was standing in a line with other inmates. I'd been told by seasoned inmates, and even by some of the guards, to keep my head down when walking past a fence where inmates already established on the yard were standing. That day, though, for one moment I looked up. An inmate on the other side shouted right at me, "Looky here!" And I did.

"Hey, you mad doggin' me, new fish?" he snarled. "This is for you," and he pointed to his crotch.

That was the last time I fell for that ploy.

Humiliation can be subtle, or it can be overt. It switches. When I first arrived in prison, those strings of barbed wire ominously perched on top of a perimeter fence filled me with a sense of humiliation. I felt caged. But within a few days of being a caged animal—and that is precisely what I was, what prisoners are—I looked at that barbed wire in a different way. It was just barbed wire, less important with every passing day.

Confinement confers an acute loss of free movement, free speech, and freedom of association, and with those losses comes the erosion of individuality. Inmates are constantly looking for breaches in security— sometimes for nefarious reasons and sometimes simply for entertainment—and they are constantly struggling against the lure of freedom. As that happens, logic and reason melt away. Additionally, administrators are constantly looking to strip away any power that might threaten the safety of staff and other inmates. One method of doing so is the prison processing system, a system expert at letting each inmate feel he is merely an article of inventory to be stored and maintained until some future date.

Dear Mom and Dad,

I'm writing to you, again, from the CTQ [holding area before being processed]. I've had another TB test (negative), been given the same reading comprehension test for the 3rd time (I always get a perfect score), had my teeth counted, again (losing one or more teeth usually translates to being involved in a fight), and now I await going to committee for classification for a job, for the third time, so I can be cleared to interact with the general public. I am powerless to say: "Hey, you have already collected my blood, my urine, counted my teeth, and given me a dozen TB tests." A fellow inmate once refused to have his inner cheek scraped for DNA harvesting (required of all inmates in California) and was threatened with a week in solitary confinement (the SHU). Powerless to divert the inevitable, he gave in and allowed the humiliating procedure to take place over the chortles of the guards.

—*Letter home, September 23, 2004*

A natural reaction to feeling powerless is to arm oneself. I won't say much about manufactured weapons fashioned by inmates on the yard. Much of this information is available in the public domain. I'll say only that they are a major concern of prison administrators and guards. Prisoners fashion weapons and hide them around the yard, in dorms, in their cells, or up their butts. They do this for two reasons: to use against guards and to use against other inmates.

Knowing the latter fact fueled an ongoing internal exercise I engaged in while in prison. Like other inmates, I was forever reminding myself of the rules of the yard, reminding myself never to deviate from what is expected of a "good inmate," good, that is, by the unwritten inmate code of respect and acceptable behavior. I didn't realize while I was inside that life in prison was similar to living under the rules dictated in my marriage, rules dictated by Melanie. Those rules restricted speech (no business talk at home), coupled with Melanie's code of conduct to do things her way or risk being punished by humiliation, shame, or total destruction. As I came to realize these similarities, I couldn't help but wonder how Melanie functioned during her two-year prison term. She was someone who considered herself in charge, and often saw herself as above the rules. I know now that anyone like that in a men's prison would be sniffed out in seconds and silenced by force.

Rats

They kept pounding his face with their boots. My instinct was to help; I know this guy. I was frozen and could not move. A crowd of 20–30 inmates circled the combatants on the side of the dorm out of sight of the guards. Combatants? Five against one is less than a fair fight. The guy with the bloodied head, crying for mercy, turned out to be a rat.

—*Journal entry, April 13, 2004*

College and law school don't have courses on how to survive prison. Before being sent into combat, soldiers are trained, their skills honed until their survival instincts are raw and close to the surface, and thus they're prepared for anything they might encounter. Soldiers train to survive against the onslaught of a known enemy. But prisoners are another thing altogether. Prisoners enter a system where the enemy is not easily known, and they enter that system with no training or preparation. The learning curve in prison is steep and up to each individual to figure out—especially how to recognize the enemy and how to navigate each day without offending someone. There's no etiquette book on prison survival because no single book could cover all the possible situations. Each individual's experience is different. And every experience inside threatens terror at any moment. In a split second an inmate's safety can vanish.

One day after I'd been incarcerated for a while, I was walking the track around the yard in Ironwood when I felt a chilling stillness around me. The air suddenly felt thick, like oxygen was being dealt out in chunks. In uneasy silence, everything seemed to move in slow motion. I could feel the anesthetizing effect of a great many human beings massing together, but I knew I needed information, fast. Questions began to pinball through my mind: What were the politics of the brewing conflict? Was this limited to two men or to two hundred men? Was there a racial overtone? Which inmates were nearest to me? What were they doing? When would I hear the belting voice over the PA system ordering us to get down—to drop flat on our stomachs, heads facing the ground?

I looked around the otherwise bustling yard and noticed no one was moving. A few inmates were pointing, and a few were slowly walking in one direction, grouping themselves into racial pods. My slow walk turned into a run as a feeling of insecurity washed over me—and over the entire yard. I felt the prison panic response I'd first felt as a new fish. I didn't always find out what was going on.

Over the years, I learned the rules of engagement for each yard where I was housed. The theme was generally the same: each of us was supposed to protect our own race. This loyalty to race was inculcated into me in my first minutes in county jail where I was housed with other whites and with Hispanics. I knew instinctively and quickly that I had to be loyal to my race, that that was a given inside. And over time I watched as this theme played out time and again in greater and greater specificity. For instance, no inmate of any race ever leaves a cell or a dorm without his boots on. There are no excuses. This rule ensures that inmates' feet are always battle ready.

On a hot August afternoon at Ironwood with the temperature hovering near 107 degrees, I wore a pair of shower flip-flops out into the yard. There a few black inmates told me in no uncertain terms that I was disrespecting "the foot combat preparedness rule" of the yard. They ushered me back into the dorm to change into my heavy, used, ill-fitting, smelly, state-issued boots. I never disobeyed that rule again, despite the heat.

Loud human noises and the thud of men pounding each other with fierce, pent-up anger usually revealed the location of whatever fight was going on. The yard's siren blared over the loudspeaker system, and the command to get down followed immediately in that piercing voice, as if Thor were speaking. Those still engaged in combat didn't get down and became easy targets for guards to identify as combatants.

The first fight after dinner is Foxx v. Wallah. Foxx is an aggressive black man who has lost his patience with this place. He and I get along well. Got his sentence reduced seven days. Wallah's top bunk is next to mine. He is new, he is soft-spoken. Wallah is a Muslim and has a Muslim Bunkie. Because he looked and acted differently, I feared for his safety. He prays five times—early evening, early afternoon, later afternoon, after sunset, and early evening. Foxx does not like the way Wallah dresses, or keeps his head down when he walks the yard.

Did not see it, but on the way back from chow I heard Foxx chide Wallah about not walking with his head down. Sounds like Foxx was the aggressor—not a surprise. Both rolled up, but Wallah returned to the same bunk later on. Foxx not returning—odd. Told Wallah I'm glad he's back and okay. It seems like he'll be treated as a rat (because

he returned and Foxx didn't). Days later, Wallah and his Bunkie were
savagely beaten when kneeling in evening prayer, rolled up and moved
to another yard never to be heard from again.

—*Journal entry, June 5, 2004*

When guards questioned me about what I had seen during any fight
on the yard, I had to offer a face that was pure deadpan, a face that said,
"Nothing." No one wants to be known as a rat, even if being one means
speaking out on behalf of what is just. I wasn't proud of not ratting in this
situation or in others, but the alternative was too threatening. Ratting
on someone identified as a rat meant I was not trustworthy. In prison,
rats are scum, lower than child molesters in the prison hierarchy. Rats
fall victim to the prisoners' own judicial system, and that system has no
statute of limitations. Being designated a rat follows an inmate for life,
follows him even back on the streets.

Prisoners view rats as pernicious threats to their safety, and rats exist
in every race. They are not suspected because of the way they act or for
the people with whom they associate. Rather, there's always a sense that
someone may do or say something that flies in the face of the prevailing inmate-enforced prison culture. This state of mind helps maintain
a chronic, low-grade tension on the yard. At one moment you could be
walking with someone you'd gotten to know only to discover he's a rat.

This happens. It happened to me. When I was at Ironwood, I
befriended a white man who, unbeknownst to me, had been labeled
a rat for telling a guard that he was being threatened over a gambling
debt by a gang member of another race. The threatening man was
swiftly rolled up and removed from the yard. Several months later, in
the middle of summer, the man I befriended and I were walking the
yard when he abruptly decided to go back into the dorm to get out of
the desert heat. I kept walking the track when I suddenly felt the atmo-
sphere on the yard turn chilly. I turned in the direction of a horrible
thudding sound and saw my friend being swarmed by members of a
gang who were pouncing on him, kicking him, bloodying his face, and
breaking his bones. I was horrified, and I couldn't move. I later learned
that the whites had given the attackers the go-ahead to enact this penalty with impunity because both whites and blacks agreed he was a rat
and thus not worth defending. A seasoned inmate once told me that if
a child molester and a rat were lined up to be shot and only one bullet

was in the chamber, he'd shoot and kill the rat and pound the molester to death with the gun. These priorities proved to be universal.

If there were an etiquette book for survival in prison, it would be a bestseller if it highlighted realities of prison life for new fish. Prison life mirrors what's going on in the streets, and prison is indeed a microcosm of the outside world—but one that is condensed in its intensity and volatility. All the social problems on the street pour into the nation's prisons and jails in lethal doses. At first new fish don't realize the toxicity of the rat poison they are about to encounter. A prison etiquette book would need a chapter entitled "Prison Survival Etiquette for New Fish," and at the top of the list would be *rats*.

Almost a decade after my time in prison, on July 17, 2013, I received a letter from an inmate who was responding to the research I was doing for this book. I had posed this question: "What skills have you used to survive in prison?"

> I have learned rules, which I guess could be considered skills: (1) Do not RAT on anyone; (2) Do not owe anybody anything, (3) Do not gamble, (4) Do not get involved with drugs, (5) Mind my own business. By living by this code I have survived.

Whistle-blowers are not recognized in prison etiquette, but prison administrators are fully aware of the onus the general population of prisoners place on snitches, whether those rats are dry or wet. A dry rat is the inmate who witnesses something on the yard that is against the rules: use of drugs, mutual combat, a planned escape, the manufacturing of pruno (an alcoholic beverage surreptitiously brewed by inmates), or an imminent threat of any kind to the guards. A dry rat offers enough information to draw attention to a situation without mentioning names or explicit details. Examples of information a dry rat might volunteer under questioning or voluntarily might include, for instance

"I smell marijuana over there by the showers."

"Officer Kelly's days are numbered."

"Security should be heightened around the perimeter tonight."

"That chump Joe, he wasn't at chow this morning."

In contrast, a wet rat gives specific information leading to the identity of one or more inmates that leads to their arrest (or bust). Some examples of a wet rat's comments might be

"Short Dog, Buddy, Windy, and Gypsy are smoking marijuana by the showers."

"The two white lead cooks on the morning shift intend to stick Officer Kelly in the morning."

"Inmate V12214 is going over the fence after chow tomorrow night."

"I seen Joe go over the fence by the sally port."

In prison parlance, a *sally port* is a secure, controlled entryway into a prison. To enter, everyone and everything, including all vehicles and inmates, is inspected for contraband.

In greater contrast still, nonrats see nothing, hear nothing, know nothing, and are never swayed from their perfect vacuum of no knowledge. Seeing nothing and hearing nothing are not, in and of themselves, criminal acts. However, if a fight breaks out on the yard and guards see combat but don't know exactly who is involved beyond those who do not drop when ordered to do so, everyone on the yard is vulnerable to a body check for cuts and bruises. I experienced fights flaring up right next to my bunk—one was a horrible fight. But when an investigator came by for a statement, he began by saying, "So you saw nothing, right Roseman?" I replied, "That's right," with an invisible wink of my eye.

The pressure to say nothing is smothering. All eyes are on the one approached by someone in authority, and others will note any hint that you might be a rat. Talking too long with a guard is suspect behavior. And beyond being seen as a rat, if an inmate gets too friendly with a staff member, the inmate can be charged by administrators with "familiarization with staff," which can result in removal from the general population pending transfer to another prison.

When fights broke out and someone was hurt, guards did weapons checks in each inmate's living area. Like all inmates, I had my knuckles checked for fresh bruises and a full body check for evidence of recent trauma. For this reason, sustaining a non-combat-related cut or bruise is a potential problem for an inmate since these blemishes may be misread. I learned early on that if I sustained an innocent cut or bruise, I had to go immediately to the medical clinic so that on-duty personnel would have that bruise or cut photographed and recorded in my chart. This procedure to ensure a not-sustained-in-combat notation can save an inmate many problems. Inside, men whose knuckles or bodies betray them with visible bruises waive their Fifth Amendment rights to self-incrimination (not that they had any anyway, inside) and often are pressured to give up more information or to do time in the hole (stripped down to shorts and remanded to solitary confinement). Whether an inmate becomes a rat and thereafter is placed in protective custody depends on an individual's constitution for confinement and administrative pressure—including such punishment as loss of mail and visitation rights. But no matter the reason for turning into a rat, the label is indelible and unforgiveable.

A dry rat may be treated as severely as a wet rat because both involve commiseration with prison authorities. The prison inmate communication system throughout California's thirty-three men's prisons and myriad county jails is efficient. The resettlement of inmates, by transfers between prisons and the constant shuffling of new inmates who are either new fish or parole violators, provides interprison and intraprison communication throughout the prison system. It's easy to find out who isn't to be trusted. The outside and inside mail systems, phone calls, and visitations also contribute to the intraprison communication system.

The US mail is delivered to prisons five days a week, and outgoing mail is collected on weekday evenings for mailing the next day. Prison guards check incoming and outgoing mail for written and physical content. Inmates can send mail only if it is unsealed, and mail received has always first been opened and then resealed with scotch tape. Still, mail is sometimes written in code—thus communicating the whereabouts of a rat without being discovered.

Everyone who has gone through the prison system learns information that could make him or her a rat. Prison makes for strong bonds between people who otherwise would never associate. In prison, my circle of friends and people of influence were far different from those of men who hailed from gang-infested neighborhoods in Los Angeles, Bakersfield, the Inland Empire, and beyond. And still, from forced bonds comes a strong brotherhood and an even stronger sense of common purpose—the primary one being survival until your EPRD, earliest possible release date. Men who have no release date form strong bonds in prison that may last all their days, or until a seemingly unprovoked and abrupt roll up and transfer to another prison.

The bonds I made inside are with me still, and I know they will be forever, but I have taken no pledges of any sort to keep secrets or protect anyone's interests on the inside. I have a connection with men who have endured incarceration, and that connection exists regardless of criminal history. In this book I tell stories, but I am not a rat. I've offered stories that are based on observation, a factual regurgitation of time-digested experiences; I tell stories anyone who has ever served time will recognize; and I have changed names and in some cases circumstances to protect the not-always innocent.

The Bus Ride to Hell

California has thirty-three men's prisons, and it is customary not to give inmates much notice about any upcoming move. Over the years I was moved with no notice beyond a shout, "Roll it up, Roseman" while I was asleep. The theory is that if an inmate knows when he'll be in transit, a phone call to someone outside could result in the hijacking of a CDCR bus, or worse. The buses all vary their routes between prisons, jails, and courthouses as a safety precaution. When I was in reception at Wasco State Prison, I had figured I'd be moved after New Year's Eve 2003—that year New Year's Eve was a Wednesday.

I figured wrong.

Being startled from sleep into the unknown is both frightening and exciting. The closest sensation I can liken it to is that moment when a roller-coaster creeps to the very top and moves into the accelerating plunge that makes you feel as if you are being forced out of your body through your mouth. That's exactly how I felt that day when I was wakened to be shipped out of Orange County Jail.

Instead, at 3:00 a.m. on December 31, 2003, I was awakened by a shout into my left ear: "Roll it up, Roseman." It took me a minute to remember where I was, something that happened a lot when I awoke in the morning. The harsh reality of where I was, was something that I learned to cope with fast. The CO (correctional officer) in charge of my unit called me to the front desk and told me to get ready for "de-processing." He didn't say when I would be moving on to my assigned prison or, for that matter, to which prison I was being assigned.

I had nothing to pack beyond prescription glasses, so I rolled up my thin mattress, made a quick bathroom run, and flew outside to the bus. I had no time to brush my teeth much less say goodbye to anyone. I was on prison time, another example of when prison did you until you could figure out how to regain control. I learned that morning I had been assigned to Ironwood State Prison in Blythe, California, a name that sounded like a golf course to me.

Many other inmates and I, about to make the ride, were rushed through the de-processing procedures: we were strip searched and our identification was checked over and over—archived photos and finger-prints—after which we each were issued a red jumpsuit that was made of a strange material and zipped from neck to navel. We were issued flip-flops as footwear, the kind with a piece that fits between the big toe and the second toe. By 4:00 a.m. it was time for breakfast, and all thirty-one of us stood in a straight line next to a wall in the commissary eating our bologna sandwiches and apples. Staff did not issue drinks. The bus was not equipped with a bathroom, and the Wasco-Blythe run is four hundred miles, a trip that would take over seven hours. We would end up in the Sonoran Desert, 225 miles east of Los Angeles, 150 miles west of Phoenix.

That was a New Year's Eve I will never forget. As the bus rolled down the streets, I saw stores bustling with people buying food and alcohol to add to their celebrations while I was heading into the unknown and facing more uncertainty about my safety and future.

There is a duplicity of tasks that slows the depressing process. Staff are required to perform repetitive tasks. They go over medical screening results, background history, gang association, tattoos, and classifica-tion background checks in small, cramped quarters that makes the experience out-of-body. I have had 4 TB tests since entering the sys-tem, all within a period of eight weeks, all negative.

The actual transfer was by bus. There were 32 of us. It was no Greyhound. The CDCR uses a separate transportation department to move its charges. They recruit from neo-Nazi underground organizations, or so it seems. The driver and the fellow in a separate cage with his loaded shotgun, were by far the meanest, most intimidating, and overtly uncaring human beings I've encountered here to date. Our 7-hour bus trip was done in mandated silence . . . and I mean NO talking, whatsoever. A violation of the silence rule (it happened twice) resulted in a barrage of verbal meanness, sharp and personal. If the punishment meted out could hurt or cause mayhem, the "verbal violators" would be dead. The turmoil it creates is keenly unsettling, and in my case, took all I had to deal with the resulting tensions and frictions on some rational level. All I came up with was: this too shall pass; this too shall become yet another memory hopefully stripped of the immediate emotional pain. Writing about it helps.

—*Letter to my sister, January 2, 2004*

What I didn't write about in that letter to my sister, but what I remember clearly, was my travel mate that day. Before we entered the bus, we all felt that chilling suspense about what was going to happen next. Guards told us not to communicate with anyone in any way. At the bus stairs, each of us had our feet shackled with a twelve-inch chain that restricted the length of our gait (we would do the "prison shuffle" to move). Our hands were cuffed with no separation and attached to a waist chain so we only had a limited upward range of hand movement—not too far beyond nose-picking logistics. We each were paired with another inmate, shoved into hard plastic seats, and our hands were locked to each other.

Before leaving Wasco and prior to being issued our jumpsuits, we had been strip-searched. By that time I had developed the ability to intentionally blunt my emotions and find mental stability in my protective shell, so the strip search was not as humiliating as it had been in the beginning of my time inside. That blunted, numb state was a safe place where my anxiety was reduced, a place where I envisioned myself sitting across from a female psychiatrist and talking about a particular stress issue. I never saw her face, only her legs, shoes, and skirt. I heard my voice talking, and I heard her response in calming, well-paced language. Her advice was to breathe and to recognize that I was in control and the system was not going to break me. She never billed me.

CDCR buses have cages inside for the guys perceived as being "really bad." Paranoia that inmates might escape while in transit is rampant, but even if the bus were to crash and open a pathway through which inmates could run, we would be easy-to-spot targets in our blazing red jumpsuits, and without shoes, how could we run with our feet shackled? The most we could do was shuffle.

My travel mate sat in the window seat; I sat on the aisle. He was a tall, black man, thin, noncommunicative, and where his left eye should have been sat a worn bloodstained ball of cotton. One look at him scared me. I couldn't say a word or react in any way that might cause attention, but a shudder ran through my whole body. I closed my eyes and pictured our family summer vacations. I filtered out the urine-laced smell of the air by breathing through my mouth. I couldn't wait to get to where we were going because I was sure it had to be much better than this.

On the way we stopped at an enormous truck stop so that the driver, shotgun number one, and shotgun number two could go to the bathroom and buy themselves food and drinks. As we sat at the truck stop, from the high vantage point on the bus my travel mate could see outside where free people were walking and talking and filling up their tanks with gas. Whenever he spotted a female—any female—he started to shiver and shake. My right hand, handcuffed to his left, also shivered and shook with his excitement. When his vibrations got out of control, he started stamping the floor of the bus and he let out low frequency moaning sounds. Drool dripped from his mouth, pooling on his red jumpsuit from his chest to his crotch. I turned to him and our three eyes met, and I grumbled so only he would hear: "Cut it out before someone hears you!"

Fortunately, he slipped back into total silence for the rest of the trip. The letter to my sister continued:

We were given a bag lunch. Our "server" was shotgun #2. He threw each of us a brown bag to be held in our laps. Contents: 2 PNB&J sandwiches and 2 apples. This is the last time I use this travel search engine!

We arrived at Ironwood about 5:00 PM. It was mid-winter dark. I felt disorientated by the lights glaring into the bus and the shouting by cops to "move out, ass-holes, we got a party to go to so MOVE!" From what I could see from the terrain, this place made the moon's surface look like a virtual floribunda. I've come to learn that there's nothing alive here that's not classified as a member of the reptilian species . . . except us unfortunate humans.

The loud hiss of the airbrakes woke me from a trance as we pulled into the lot in front of Ironwood. Guards hustled us quickly off the bus and relieved us of our chains and restraints—what relief! Guards then reprocessed us, rephotographed us *seven times* for new ID cards, and gave each of us the by-then routine TB skin test. We were strip-searched and given a brief verbal orientation of the prison by a friendly cop holding a not-so-friendly rifle. We were rushed through so the shift could leave and celebrate the dawning of 2004.

At the orientation reprocessing we each were paired with another inmate to share a two-man cell. Guards handed us a pillowcase that held the quintessential orange jumpsuit, a pair of flip-flops, two white T-shirts, and a pair of white socks. We each received a bag filled with sundry hygiene products, referred to as *state issue*: a four-inch tooth-brush, toothpaste that smelled like plaster of Paris and had the same consistency when mixed with water, and soap that burned the skin when mixed with water. We were not issued razorblades for obvious reasons. We shaved during our showers, which lasted five minutes three times a week. Before the shower we received a razor and afterward we returned it. If a razor went missing, the entire yard went on lockdown until the missing razor was found.

The guards explained we would spend a short time in twenty-four-hour lockdown, in two-man cells, until we were classified or until we had met with a committee of prison personnel who would screen us for our job assignments. After that we would be moved to a designated yard. Eventually I was assigned to A-yard, a level I yard.

In California prisons, there are four levels. Level I is the lowest secu-rity and has ten-foot chain-link perimeter fences. Level II is similar but with rolled barbed wire on top of the perimeter fences. Level III is cellblock living, mainly two-man cells where inmates spend most of the day locked in a cell. Level IV prisons are high security, like San Quentin, California's highest security prison opened in July 1852 and containing the state's only death row.

This ride to Ironwood was just one of the many bus rides I took to hell and back for the two years I was incarcerated by the California Department of Corrections. To this day, whenever I see an unmarked CDC bus with its distinct light-and-dark-green colors, I react viscer-ally—the air is sucked out of my body and my chest and limbs tighten. In fact, the sight of any bus shaped like a CDC transport, whether commercial or private, triggers a visceral memory of those hard molded-plastic seats, the smell of sweat and rot, and the fear that was to be my daily companion until my return to freedom.

CHAPTER FIVE

Surviving Culture Shock

It's not true: sticks and stones can break my bones, but words can never harm me.

—*Journal entry, February 19, 2005*

G OING TO PRISON IS like traveling to a faraway country and encountering a brand-new culture. Everything is unfamiliar—from the language and food to the customs and rituals—but you have to learn fast if you're going to survive.

Language and Nuance

Like all languages, prison lingo adopts slang shortcuts so understanding the precise meaning of someone's words requires knowing the way words and phrases are nuanced or assigned subtle differences in color, meaning, or feeling. Getting it wrong, in prison, can be fatal. If an inmate is told he's a *Maytag* and he thinks he's hearing a joke about a washing machine, he's in trouble—he's actually being told he's someone who won't be able to protect himself from prison rape. A Maytag is someone who has been marked as vulnerable prey. And so in addition to all the other things I had to adjust to, I had to learn prison language, which is why I kept an ever-growing lexicon of prison jargon in one of my journals.

When read out of context, my list of common words and phrases of daily prison life seems trite and silly now, but back then staying out of trouble meant learning the language and applying it in appropriate circumstances. One example is the courtesy flush. When I first heard the phrase, I thought it related to poker, and not being a card player, I presumed it had no application to me. I learned the hard way that the gerund form—*courtesy flushing*—meant the strategic flushing of the toilet to reduce odors from spreading through the nonpartitioned common toilet area. When once I violated the courtesy flush rule, I was called out by a member of the *white car*—as the Caucasian prison population is collectively known—and that was humiliating. I had failed to flush to create an odor barrier; it takes practice to coordinate the move, but after the first time, it never happened again. I look back at the journals and remember so many things, but what follows is a list of some of the common slang used daily, followed by the definitions and examples of proper use:

- *Don't trip:* don't get upset; don't be bothered: relax. Carl borrowed your pen, but don't trip, he'll return it. Expected response: I'm not trippn'.

- *Dawg:* trusted friend based on a shared prison experience. Mike's my dawg from when we did time together at Ironwood. Likewise, that makes me Mike's dawg.

- *Shoot it:* send it (usually contraband) to me; share it with me. If you're eating your apple, shoot it (to me). Past tense usage: I shot it (the apple).

- *Break me off:* give me some, share that with me. Break me off some of the cake. Past tense usage: I broke off some cake for him.

- *Car:* designation of race. He runs (associates) with the white car.

- *Holder of the keys to the car:* the inmate who has the final say on important issues relating to his race's involvement in risking conduct on the yard. Also known as *the shot caller*. Gerry was the shot caller for the black car before being transferred to San Quentin. Fred is the holder of the keys to the black car.

- *Wood:* Caucasian. Derogatory word used by other cars. He runs with Woods, aka *Woodpeckers*.

- *Program:* an inmate's daily routine. My program is wake up, go to chow, work in the library, write letters, walk the yard, go to chow, walk the yard, and go to bed. Past tense usage: I was finally programmed after waiting to be classified (approved) for working in the library.

- *The hole:* solitary confinement, aka segregated housing unit (SHU). When the drug-sniffing dog found his stash of hash, he was rolled up (possessions removed from the yard) and put in the hole.

- *Count:* aka the count of every inmate on the yard. Throughout the California prison system, the count is done five times a day at the same time each day. If the count is off by a single inmate, the entire prison system shuts down until the missing person is accounted for.

- *OG:* original gangster. An inmate who has served multiple prison terms. An *OG* is not necessarily an older inmate. *OGs* get respect for their prison tenure.

- *New fish:* a new arrival on the yard. All *new fish* receive a *fish kit* consisting of state-issued hygiene sundries. Most new fish trash their fish kit in exchange for commercial products purchased from the canteen.

- *A 115:* the form used by CDCR for making a rules violation report. Staff members[1] who think an inmate broke a rule have fifteen days from the date of discovery of the infraction to write him a 115 and issue him his copy. The administration has thirty days from that point to have a hearing. The result of a successful 115 can be an extended sentence. For fighting during the ballgame, Jose's punishment was sixty days tacked onto his sentence.

- *A 602:* the form used by inmates for an administrative appeal to complain about an action taken by any employee of the CDCR or any CDCR policy or procedure that affects the prisoner. Examples are medical care delays, failure to follow procedural rules for disciplinary violation hearings, miscalculation of work credits, restrictive mail policies, or visitor denials.

- *But a minute:* when an inmate's remaining sentence is under a year. Aka *short.* With only nine months to serve, Jesse was short; he'll be on the yard *but a minute.*

- *Don't get that twisted*: don't lie, tell the truth. Your version of what happened is wrong; don't get that twisted if you know what's good for you. Used interchangeably with *that's a cold piece of work*. That story he told the lieutenant was a cold piece of work. This expression is also used with *talking smack*. I saw what you did; stop talking smack. A similar usage is *flip the script*: lying. You got that twisted—don't flip the script on me. We also have *miss me with that*: cut the bullshit. I told him to miss with that crap about having a PhD in astrophysics.

- *Off the hook:* amazingly good. The Christmas dinner was off the hook! This is synonymous with *the bomb*.

- *Pop the clutch:* I'm tired of you, pop the clutch.

A Word about *Fuck*

There were times when inmates' dexterous use of the word *fuck* made me dizzy. In a prison setting, *fuck* is one of the most varying and interchangeable words (just a notch above *shit*). It's packaged in many forms, taking on the guise of a verb, noun, adjective, expression of pain, or space filler when the right word escapes the speaker's grasp.

Fuck is often used with spitting, before or after. The word is emphasized by repetition, and usage determines the appropriate body language to exaggerate the word. The tone used when telling someone to "get the fuck outta here" will match the body language appropriate at that moment. *Fuck* has its own international hand and finger sign language we all learned early in life.

Over time, I came to hate the word no matter how it was used. I heard it over and over, preceded by a full spit and followed by the grabbing of the spitter's own genitals. I looked forward to the Jewish chaplain's weekly visits to the yard. During our talks, he did not say *fuck* or any of its derivatives. He used clean, fresh sounding English with a slight Yiddish accent, and his calm and considered use of the language calmed me.

While in prison, I learned the power of language and that the bastardization of the English language brought me stress—who would have thought? To this day, whenever I hear gratuitous foul language, I feel a twinge run up my spine. Sometimes I have flashbacks to cramped holding cells and times when my insides squirmed and I longed to get far away from the verbal polluters. Thankfully, the passage of time has softened the blow of an unexpected *fuck this* or a *fuck that*. I'm equally grateful that the accompanying spitting and crotch squeezing isn't prevalent on the outside.

No matter the limerick, words can cause harm.

Survival

> I don't fit in, but for survival purposes, I have associated, tangentially and sometimes directly, with the power "Homeys" who watch out for me when growing tensions mount.
>
> —*Letter to my parents, November 2003*

Wasco, California, was my introduction to the California penal system. I lived in the freestanding dormitory setting; the more serious offenders lived in cells. The dorm was one-quarter the size of a Costco, the ceiling maybe fifty feet high. The dorms were well ventilated with temperatures hovering around sixty-five degrees. The room was separated in half, and in the middle was the day room, the place where prisoners watched television and during chowtime ate meals. All the seats and tables were stainless steel riveted to the cement floor. There were no windows. Guards sat on a podium in the middle of the room and communicated using a PA system.

Before catching the chain to Wasco, in my eight weeks at OCJ, I had learned a lot about state-sanctioned, hard-core racial discrimination. On a chow line we queued up by race: whites, English-speaking Mexicans, and Spanish-speaking Mexicans. I never saw a black or Asian in a chow line. In the mess hall, which was open to outside observation, the races were mixed. At OCJ, I learned that whites and Mexicans can share a cell or a tiered bunk, and blacks and "others" (Asians, Muslims, and people with unrecognizable accents) were housed together. At the mainline prison, eating arrangements were segregated by race.

From OCJ to Wasco, every day was one more day of having survived. The danger was seldom directly in front of me. The real danger was in not knowing what was going on. Stress and anxiety flowed from hypervigilance—I, like every inmate, lived with my raw animal instincts primatively coded to preserve health and life. In prison the fittest don't always survive. There are no rules of engagement, and the end is justified once a means exists. It doesn't take much to trigger the fight-or-flight mechanism in the body that enables humans to quickly mobilize a lot of energy for coping with perceived threats to survival. Prison parallels the operation of businesses, governments, and war. Humans naturally order and govern themselves, whether they're men on a prison yard, children on a schoolyard or business partners in a conference room. Inmates, I quickly learned, feel the natural need to order and categorize themselves apart from governmental authorities that hold them in captivity and from other inmates who are different from their street-bred associates. Details are checked and rechecked. I never got over the fact, for instance, that at reception every inmate must designate where his body is to be shipped if he dies inside.

We humans are a herding species, and forced fraternal confinement sorts us into herds that forage together. Because herding is systemic in human development, I wasn't surprised to see social problems born on the street marinating in prison. In prison, the drug addicts, social outcasts, illiterates, and those suffering medical and mental-health problems stew, so prison becomes a world of contained anarchy. The state controls the perimeters, but contained human beings will create their own operating procedures within those perimeters, including systems of justice and reward. No inmate is an instant comrade; each individual earns his position by grouping with those of like mind or by standing out while taking care not to be perceived as different or threatening.

I quickly learned to play the ghost role well. Only when I sensed that showing more of who I was would not potentially be harmful did I open up, and then only a bit. Sometimes I opened up to one man at a time, testing the waters. I would walk up to someone and introduce myself as Jewish and a former lawyer, but that usually was too much information. I quickly realized that, in a sense, meeting other inmates was as delicate as going on a first date. I had to reveal little pieces of myself slowly and gauge the other's reaction before I could risk peeling back another layer of my personal onion.

Upon arrival on a yard, every inmate is suspect, everyone is a new fish. Are you a member of a rival gang? Are you someone others will want to kill or are you someone who kills? New fish also arouse a rush for the inmates already on the yard; the numbing boredom of prison is momentarily suspended when new fish arrive. Are you packing (smuggling in tobacco, drugs, sharp objects, or whatever else can fit up your butt)? New fish sometimes bring messages that change lives—the lives of inmates as well as the lives of prison staff.

But no yard offers new fish a handbook on how things run, and so I had to quickly learn that every yard has a holder of the keys to the car, the guy most highly respected within each of the separate races on that yard. *Car* means *race,* and whites are called *woods*, *woodpeckers*, or *peckers*, for short. I learned in an intriguing twist of social/anthropological order that the Woods don't consider Aryan Brotherhood and skinheads part of the white race. Skinheads and the Aryan Brotherhood have no race distinction other than their separatist classification. Mexicans also have a clear line of demarcation between their northern (norte) and southern (sur) classifications. A fierce, warlike hatred exists between the two, the reasons for which are beyond the scope of this book.

Experienced inmates and observation taught me what I needed to know about prison race divisions. I quickly understood that there were four cars in California prisons: white, black, Mexican, and other (that included Asians and Samoans). The holder of the key to every car was the ultimate decision maker for that car, and the car key holders had lieutenants who met the new fish at the sally port where inmates were loaded off the bus and received their photo ID cards.

That card is important; it's the inmate's only form of photo identification. Driver's licenses, credit cards, photos, and all other tangible connections to the outside are considered contraband, taken away from each new fish, and sent home. At the sally port, the key holder gave the new fish a general overview of the yard—describing current racial relations, politics, bathroom etiquette, who had tobacco, who did tattooing, whom to avoid, and where the new fish's bunk assignment is. When I was assigned to Ironwood, I learned fast that the holder of the keys to the white car was a big, burly man nicknamed Tiny. He resembled Dan Blocker, the actor who played Hoss Cartwright on *Bonanza*. Tiny was soft-spoken and mild mannered, but he kept the white car in order with his keen ability to lead. He had been a ranch hand in Bakersfield in Kern County, and when I met him he was serving seven years for a barroom assault and battery. He was burning out in his leadership role since he knew he had only eighteen months to go. He had a twinkle in his eye and a good sense of humor, and he liked me. He told me I was a good stabilizing force for the car, and he taught me a lot about prison politics. He's the first person who explained I should never be seen alone talking to a guard for more than thirty seconds or the other inmates would wonder what we were talking about. He told me never to argue with anyone in another car. "Bring them issues to me," he said, "and I'll deal with 'em."

In dorms, the race key holders make the bunk assignments, and this perpetuates the racial segregation rampant in California prisons. This policy was part of the United States Supreme Court case *Johnson v. California,* discussed in greater detail in chapter 6.[2] New fish, I learned, are never assigned a top bunk.In cases of triple bunks (which happened due to overcrowding), the top bunk was the prize since the lower and middle bunks have just a few inches of space between your face and the bottom of the upper bunk. Those with physical problems who require priority bunking need a doctor's note if they ever hope to score a bottom bunk. Otherwise, bed assignments change as inmates are transferred or when the lucky ones are set free. A system of seniority plus who you know determines who moves when and where.

Wasco State Prison was a colorless world, varying in shades of gray. Bright and iridescent colors were confined to inmates' jumpsuits. Wasco, like all other prisons, had no wall decorations beyond those signs that stated "Warning Shots Are Not Fired Inside," and, "No Smoking." Of all the ironies, the most striking was that Wasco sat in a bed of roses; 55 percent of all roses grown in the United States are grown in the rich soils in and around Wasco. But inside, beyond the fact that there was no color, no carpet, nothing visually soft, there were no soft places to sit. The yards had cement benches; waiting areas had hard wooden benches; even the library had hard rigid wooden chairs. In prison décor, cushions are an unknown, and walls feature only graffiti and pornography.

When I met Tiny, he explained the reason behind the color restriction. Gang colors, he told me, are like the flags of warring nations and evoke strong fight-or-flight emotions. Clashing colors on a yard can lead to a jumping off, prison slang for a riot. Colors in prison mean loyalty, honor, common cause. Gangs do not honor each other's colors. And so, prison erases them all.

Survival comes in many forms. Breathing oxygen is a cornerstone in Abraham Maslow's hierarchy of needs[3] and sometimes in prison it was the survival issue of the day. When I first arrived at Ironwood, the air didn't smell right. It smelled stale, recycled, with a hint of industrial oil in the ventilated air that was pumped into the tiny cells through a small vent on the wall. The cells were enclosed with no bars, and depending on the structural configuration of the cellblock, the only cell window was a narrow thick Plexiglas fourth wall that had a door cut into it that led to the day room of the cellblock. Without air pumping in, we had no other source of oxygen in our cells. Next to that small vent was another vent, a return vent that sucked the air back out of the cell. This mechanical diaphragm was the lifeline inmates recognized they needed for survival. Each night that I lay on my bunk listening to the rhythmic rushing in and sucking out of the mechanical diaphragm, I knew the air was keeping me alive.

And then one night it happened, my greatest fear: power failure. It was after midnight when the flowing in and sucking out stopped. My cellmate was asleep, and I listened to each breath he took—each breath competing with the breaths I needed for survival. I caught myself before I descended into full panic. I did not wake my cellie, thinking that if he woke, he would breathe more deeply and thus require more oxygen. I had the buried-alive-in-a-coffin prison panic attack, and I lay as still as I could, going to places in my mind where fresh air existed. I went to the beach in Maui. I went to my grandparents' home on Lake Mahopac, New York. I knew what was going on, but knowing something intellectually doesn't stop it from happening.

A prison panic attack is an involuntary and uncontrollable reaction to prison containment. It usually happens at night when you're not thinking about it, when the raw reality of confinement meshes with the real sense of helplessness. The result is time doing you. That night the words of the Original Gangster from Orange County Jail never stopped reverberating in my mind. Fear compounded the real difficulty of breathing. When that air stopped pumping, the scent of air thick with an oil-based lubricant triggered within me the insurmountable desire to run, but I was aware of the walls and obstacles surrounding me. Still, my drive to run through those walls, past the gates and towers, and to race for miles to a safe place, was bursting inside me.

I stumbled down from my top bunk, held my chest to keep my heart from pounding out through my ribs, and began to pace: four and a half steps one way, four and a half steps the other way. I did this for what seemed like hours, though in fact it was, we were told later, forty-one minutes. Each set of paces picked up in tempo as my body raged in caged fury. Eventually the charge from the panic trickled out of my nerves, and I climbed up to my bunk, my body drenched in sweat, waiting for the freeing embrace of sleep.

Before oxygen began rushing in the air vent, and before the walls caved in, I heard a rumbling mechanical heave, and the lifeline was back. Forty-one minutes had passed, and during those forty-one minutes I tapped into survival skills I had never used as an adult. My mind found self-transcending, mystically extrinsic places to soften the harsh prism of my actual world. I dived into the opposite of a prison panic, into prison hibernation, slowing my mind and body functions.

But I would learn that wasn't the most frightening moment. Guards can intentionally withhold air, and once back in Orange County Jail I experienced such an act of cruelty. In August of 2004 I sat in a holding cell waiting to testify in Melanie's case. The room was a strange shape, bars on the front cell wall, gang graffiti scrawled on walls, the ubiquitous stainless-steel toilet in the corner. The holding cell was in a hallway leading to the transportation sally port where prison buses belched their stale diesel fumes into the halls. The holding cells were made entirely of cement. In the August heat, the insulation provided some relief. On that day, in the late afternoon, I was crammed with 110 other men into a holding cell built to hold eighty. The cement benches were covered with inmates sitting and sleeping. Others were on the cement floor, resting and sleeping in myriad configurations, using sneakers as pillows.

In a holding cell, time passes in slow, incremental measurements of changing shadows, changing of guards, and the pang of hunger deep in the belly. A great many of the men in the cell were Mexican, and one young man began to lead the others in Spanish songs. The music was light and fun, lifting everyone's spirits, but suddenly a white guard appeared at the front of the cell, ran his baton over the bars, and shouted, "Shut the fuck up; you're not in Mexico, and I don't want to hear that shit." The English speakers in the group stopped singing. The non-English speakers started to sing, again: "Habia una vez un barco chiquito"[4] and the guard reappeared, red faced, rattling his key chain until he found the key to the cell door.

The sound of the sliding door brought all of us to attention. Doors that open in confinement are truly worth noticing since they signal that something is going to happen, that change is coming.

The guard, accompanied by a few other male and female white guards, ordered us to walk down a short hallway into the women's holding-cell area. The sign above the door read "Maximum Capacity: 35." All one hundred plus of us crammed into this smaller, graffiti-marred room with its single Plexiglas window to the outside and one sliding door. There were no other windows; it was just this odd-shaped holding cell encased in cement. Quickly the air grew heavy, and I heard the offended guard through the Plexiglas, his voice cruel and condescending, "See how you like it without air conditioning—you fuckers won't be singing no more."

I looked up fast. What? He wasn't going to shut off the air! In my mind's eye I envisioned World War II concentration-camp-bound box-cars stuffed so thick with people no one could lie down. We were shoulder to shoulder, and cool air continued to pump into the room, but hungry lungs sucked harder for something to breathe. Soon the chirp of the air conditioning system fell silent. I took shallow, rapid breaths, and within moments a haze fell over my oxygen-deprived mind. I kneeled and put my nose to the concrete floor to try to inhale some of the cooler, fresher air there. In minutes, all the men were on the ground seeking oxygen. A few passed out. Others kneeled in prayer. Beads of condensation covered the ceiling and the Plexiglas as we starved for oxygen. I fantasized about garnering magical strength and ripping apart that confining cement to get to air!

I heard the keys again, and a head poked into the doorway. A rush of fresh air seeped into the cotton-candy air in the room. I could hear the guards laughing. "Ever see such a mob of pussies?" one chortled, and a few minutes later we were handcuffed with our hands in front of us and hustled onto buses. As my mind cleared a little—still numb from the experience—I began to understand the unchecked power of the guards. It could be deadly. I had no time to think about lodging a complaint. The moment I returned to the stone-cold jail cell, I was focused again only on survival.

I also learned early on in my incarceration about being a *homey*. The word is sort of a contraction for *home boy*, describing the common thread between groups of inmates. A white inmate is not necessarily my homey; something more has to link us. The link might be geographical—white boys from San Diego or Los Angeles or the Inland Empire. But geography does not assure friendship. Gangs might share a neighborhood, but they can be rivals; white inmates who hold a certain philosophy—skinheads for instance—would not be my homeys. The relationships become complex. Whites and Mexicans can be homeys, but blacks can be homeys only with other blacks. *Homey* is a salutation: "Hey, homey, whatz up?" It's a designation: "He's my homey." It's a telegraphed message that your back is covered: "You touch my homey and you're dead."

Because of my age (I was in my mid-50s), my religious heritage (Jewish), and my having been a lawyer, achieving homey-hood was tricky for me but also was something that equated to survival. I understood how critical it was. In prison, older guys are vulnerable because they tend not to herd into groups or organized gangs. But anyone not associated with a group, who has no homey association, is suspect. If you want to be alone or spend more time "surfing" your bunk, reading a book, and not interacting with other inmates, you're going to be talked to by the power homey, the holder of the keys to the car. This happened to me twice. One day I was lying on my bunk in Ironwood when a serious voice asked to come on my street—that is, the space next to my bunk. I said, "Sure."

"How you doing, bro'?" he asked.

"Okay, adjusting."

"Adjusting to what?"

"You know, prison life."

"So whatta ya here for; what's your crime?"

"White collar stuff."

"How come you're a lawyer and got convicted?"

"I pled to grand theft of my clients' money."

"Where are your papers?"

"Papers?"

"Commitment papers. I wanna verify what you just said."

"Here."

I handed him the abstract of my judgment, the official court record that highlighted the precise penal code section of my conviction.

"All right, bro', all right! You realize that we gotta keep this place clean of any child molesters or rapists. Just checking."

This experience was my personal entrée into the criminals' prison justice system. I learned in that single encounter that the nature of one's crime and the supportive paperwork can be a matter of life, death, or, at a minimum, maiming. I learned an important lesson about networking within my car—there is strength in numbers, and sometimes strength in numbers is what counts.

Food

> My favorite breakfast is creamed beef aka SOS. I eat it prison style: mix the diced potatoes in with the SOS, and crumble up the biscuit into the mix, stir, enjoy!
>
> —*Letter home, August 2005*

One of the questions people outside most frequently ask me is, "How was the food?" The simple answer is that it keeps you alive.

Inmates live on a low-caloric diet, just enough to fill them up for a while, but not enough to keep gnawing hunger from quickly creeping up. Being hungry was a given most of the time, which raised the fundamental issue of survival—food and food sources are always on inmates' minds, and of course there are no refrigerators or cupboards to raid.

You haven't lived until you have had beans and pancakes for breakfast. I know such a concoction sounds filling, but the portions were curiously small and the high starch content burned off within an hour. A typical daily menu might sound good, even appetizing. Chicken was a constant staple as were beans and rice. I came up with a shorthand system that, at a glance, sheds some reality on the actual edibility factor for each course. A plus sign (+) meant *good*, a minus sign (-) meant *bad*, GW meant *give away*, SBI meant *sounds better than it is*, and HNC meant *hold nose and chew*. As an example, I might rate a typical dinner menu as follows:

- Coleslaw, 4 oz. tongs: (+)
- Kung Pao chicken, 6 oz. ladle (-) (GW) (HNC)
- Steamed rice, vegetable, 4 oz. ladle (SBI)
- Cake, iced, 1 square ea. (+)

One lunch item I always gave a minus was hoagy lunchmeat. The green iridescent hue of the composite was a turnoff. When I worked as a meat inspector in Ohio, I'd seen how sausage was made, and the stuff we were given in prison looked like the worst combination ever: head cheese and blood pudding. When hungry enough to eat the lunchmeat,

I used lots of mustard and nose-closed breathing to enable me to inhale whatever nutrition there was.

Inmates are prohibited from having bills or coins, the theory being that money will encourage gambling, and gambling encourages disputes, and disputes cause fights, and fights can escalate to jumping offs. Food is not permitted to be smuggled out of the chow hall. Guards watched us all as we entered, while we ate, and as we exited. We had twelve minutes to eat and exit, but outside the hall, food, like drugs and frontal nudity pornography, was contraband. I learned, from other inmates, methods of slipping an apple or biscuit into my sock or in my crotch, and those apples were great for late-evening snacks when an empty, rumbling stomach growled to be fed.

And there were the goats. Goats are the human garbage cans who eat anything others don't want. These supergastrointestinal disposals of leftovers would, with permission, slop my ladle of Kung Pao chicken onto their trays, mix it with another inmate's iced carrot cake and rice, and steadfastly chow down the resultant mélange. Goats, usually wide-bodied men, paid back by leaving the donor alone on the yard. There were subtle obligations to keep feeding your goat once you'd fed him—not doing so was considered disrespectful, and in prison disrespect means trouble.

There are three legitimate ways to get more food in prison: canteen, packages, and pizza day. Canteen is a weekly event for those with money on their books, money provided by family and friends who send cashier's checks to the prison. Inmates are afforded a maximum amount they can use each week, and many inmates have no one to put money on their books. Their inevitable hunger is quenched through barter and the offer of services such as sewing, washing clothing, or tattooing, or in exchange for smuggled food.

On the yard, canteen workers are among the chosen. Supervised by just one civilian prison employee hired by the state, the opportunity for self-indulgence and smuggling allowed for easy pickings. Lines are long on canteen day, but if you are a homey of a canteen worker, you get priority and special handling. The same goes for laundry workers—homeys get sheets without pilled surfaces, blankets without holes, towels without suspect stains, and pillowcases with only one opening for inserting the pillow. Nepotism runs wild in prison, and inmates learn quickly not to complain unless a racial issue brews. White laundry workers would never dig around in a laundry cart to find an exceptionally good item of bedding for a black or other; to do so would be a form of racial heresy that could and did lead to severe reprimands by the white car.

All inmates must work, if physically able, and their pay goes on their books, minus one-third if restitution is owed to victims or for court costs. An inmate who makes nine cents an hour, minus one-third for restitution, must work about three and a half hours to earn enough for a two-dollar tube of toothpaste. Sundry items are not discounted in prison canteens, and choices are limited.

Taking food out of the chow hall is prohibited because inmates have an extraordinary ability to improvise. Any fruit properly fermented with any sugar-based product in combination with a yeast product—a biscuit or a slice of bread—could be used to create a batch of pruno, the prison version of wine. The brew is fermented in plastic garbage bags and stored in places out of sight and out of mind, such as in the back of a locker or in a hole in a low ceiling. The giveaway is the rancid alcohol odor, a cross between the smell of sugar donuts and dead rats.

But in prison, pruno, along with homemade vodka made from potatoes, is the drink of choice on weekends. I never tasted pruno because I could not get past the smell, and the high alcoholic content (wood alcohol) is known to be risky and can lead to blindness or even death. One Friday night during my time at Ironwood, three inmates on the yard were medivacked by helicopter because of alcohol poisoning. Guards rapidly spread the word that two had died before reaching the hospital.

Another food source, without the potential negative rebound, was connecting with chow hall workers. Prisons use inmate labor and free labor (noninmate) to prepare and serve inmates their food. Being on the good side of one of these guys meant a good possibility of having an opportunity to consume more calories. At Ironwood I had such a connection who was nicknamed *Duke of Earl*. The Duke was free to bring any extra food out of the commissary, which he did haphazardly. He would deliver the food in a plastic bag, mixed together. One delivery I'll never forget contained pink frosted yellow cake squares, green beans, boiled carrots, and a dollop of watery beef stew. I longed for home-cooked meals.

Another source of food—packages—was a lifeline to life outside. We were allowed to receive one package a quarter. Because of constant security concerns, packages could originate only from selected, prison-approved venders. Even books had to be sent via an approved Internet company or directly from a publisher. These precautions were put in place because drugs, needles, full frontal pornography, and God knows what else might otherwise be secreted in packages sent inside. Even letters with stickers, such as return address labels, were prohibited and returned to sender; the argument was that any number of controlled substances might be affixed to the back of a sticker, including traces of cocaine or methamphetamine. Interestingly, postage stamps, stickers themselves, were not prohibited because they are federal government issued. My guess is that as a result the Feds may be adding to the transport of drugs into our prisons.

Inmates filled out package request forms and sent them to people outside who placed our orders by phone or online. Some inmates managed to get around the one-package-per-quarter rule by having packages sent to a trusted friend who wasn't expecting a package that quarter. In consideration of the favor, the named recipient inmate would receive a kickback in the form of a hefty sampling of the package contents. And package day was like Christmas, a day of joy and a day when the gifts that arrived also conferred on the recipients some power and respect.

Whenever I received a package, I was like a kid. Early in the day, a list of those inmates receiving packages that day was posted in the dorms, and like children we waited for those lists.

The packages my parents and friends sent me felt like treasures—I received books sent directly from publishers; they had to be soft-cover to avoid providing a venue for planting drugs (like could be done in the binding of hardcovers). I received fresh white T-shirts and sunglasses and sometimes food. An inmate with a package had the power to ask and receive favors and was able to make valuable trades for contraband. A ten-ounce bag of corn chips might, for instance, satisfy a gambling debt or purchase tobacco or marijuana, and goodies in packages also broke the monotony of flavorless food—food without spices, sugar, or salt. As a result, ramen soup packages were the universal currency in prison. The salt and flavorings was an addiction for some and a food staple for most. A Cajun shrimp flavor ramen was easy to make—add boiling water from personal cookers inmates could purchase and keep by their bunks—and get ready for a feast for the taste buds. Need your clothes washed? Two soups.

Most of the items inmates ordered were coffee, ready-to-eat soups and meats, chips, cookies and crackers, peanut butter and jelly, skin-care items, shaving products, clothing, watches, and writing paper. As with most things in prison, there were limitations. The weight of the package must not exceed 480 ounces (thirty pounds). All clothing and footwear had to be white because gangs adopt certain colors as their own and wearing the wrong color can cause an offender to be stripped of his garments or physically attacked.

Package days coordinated with *spread days*, festive occasions such as holidays, birthdays, or any old Friday night. Spreads particularly attracted goats. To make a spread, inmates filled a large plastic garbage bag with an array of food substances that didn't necessarily make sense. The base ingredient was ramen noodle soup—pour boiling water from a Styrofoam cup into the dry mix containing the crunchy, freeze-dried stuff. Then add anything: sardines, bread, chocolate cake, chips, seasoning, or whatever else an inmate has offered to secure his portion of the spread. Opening the spread after it has "cooked" was like unveiling a sacred find. Shares were doled out into drinking cups, cupped hands, or taco shells and scooped up with tortilla chips if dipping rights were granted. I usually avoided spreads unless I was really hungry.

A small number of Jews populated the California prison system, but if an inmate could convince the Jewish chaplain that he sincerely held a religious belief in the Jewish dietary laws, under the Religious Land Use and Institutionalized Persons Act of 2000, he would receive kosher meals. The same was true for Muslims with regard to halal food, those foods permissible for Muslims to eat or drink under Islamic shari'ah (law). I didn't request kosher meals because I didn't consider myself to sincerely hold the beliefs as warranted by the law. Also, I had memories of terrible kosher meals on airlines, and I figured if they were bad on airplanes, they couldn't be good in prison.

But one Passover, the Jewish chaplain gave me several boxes of matzos to take back to my dormitory. Anyone familiar with this cracker-like food knows that matzos are bland and lack excitement, but not these matzos. When I carried the boxes into the dorm, I created quite a stir. Word got around fast that "Lawya"—my prison name—had something unusual to eat, and a dozen inmates with wonder in their eyes and hunger pangs in their stomachs followed me to my bunk. The "Jew bread" as they affectionately dubbed it, was manna from the rabbi.

Even Rocky, the big black homey in the corner, with little ears and a missing front tooth noticed my matzos: "Hey Lawya, what ya got dare?" he gently asked.

I told him what I had.

"What do they taste like?" His eyes moved back and forth heavy with wonderment.

I handed him a taste sample.

"Oh, it's a cracka," commented Rocky. "Looks like a big host from church," he grumbled.

Rocky declined a second sample and lumbered to his prized corner bunk, shrouded himself in blankets and towels, to continue doing whatever he does in his virtual cave.

—*Journal entry, April 18, 2005*

Ironwood, where I was housed on a minimum security yard did have one food benefit: pizza day. To qualify for a pizza day, the yard had to have been free of lockdowns and brewing tensions. The latter was a matter of degrees; there's always tension when three hundred fifty to four hundred men are housed in quarters designed to house two hundred, but degrees of tension are relative to the mercurial nature of the prison-yard environment.

The veterans' group sponsored my yard's pizza extravaganza. A local chain store was authorized to bring in boxes of previously ordered pizzas and soft drinks. I had never thought I would miss carbonation, but the tasty warmth of carbonated drinks combined with taste-bud-bursting spiced cheese and toppings was, in two words, orally orgasmic. These special days happened infrequently; in my twenty-five months of incarceration we had two pizza days.

I purchased a meat-eaters pizza and twelve pack of Coke. Shared with guys who drooled in sad envy. I had one piece for myself, but Iggy gave me two of his that paid off his self-declared can of tuna obligation to me for reading his divorce papers to him and explaining that his wife wanted out of their marriage. Gave those pieces to office clerk in exchange for two pens.

—*Journal entry, June 18, 2005*

Food was the universal, noncontraband exchange—a commodity that gained favors, paid debts, and engendered goodwill between inmates, who were usually in hunger mode. Interestingly, by the end of pizza day, when every scrap of food and ounce of soda was gone, I had an unexpected reaction—emptiness. I desperately missed the freedom of having food that's available on the streets. This reaction was strong and all consuming. With my stomach full of food I could get on the street, my mind turned to thoughts of outside, and once again time did me. The excitement of the spicy food and the carbonated fizzle poured memories into my head of movie theaters, parties at work, and calling in for a pizza on cold and snowy nights. Bam! Distress and mental anguish kicked me in the heart, and to escape from those feelings I turned to what I always did: writing letters, reading, walking around the track, listening to music, or taking a midday nap.

Time can do you, and when it does, feelings of hopelessness and loneliness set in fast. I discovered early it was best not to dwell on the outside, not to think too deeply about family and holidays and who the girl left behind might be with. I was amazed to discover the way tasty food allowed the time to creep in and do me when I wasn't watching. Of course, no one inside talked about this, but I knew others felt it, too. I observed it even in those who did not make the connection themselves.

Christmas, for instance, was an unusual day, a day when time did us all, even the Jews. Christmas Eve was eerie. The program changed, and whenever the program changed, there was temporary excitement, but it seldom lasted. Christmas Eve chow was special: turkey and ham, stuffing, yams, double vegetables, spice cake, and an extra five minutes to eat. The evening was quieter than usual, though the television still blared into the early morning. But on Christmas the content was different—no sirens wailing from cop shows and crime-based dramas. And Christmas morning was weird. The noise level in the dorm lowered. Competing radios pumped English and Spanish songs of the season into the whir of shower and bathroom sounds. People made less eye contact than usual, so many heads looked down at the ground, even when exchanging traditional Christmas greetings. At Christmastime and Easter and on three-day weekends, the Fourth of July, Thanksgiving, and New Year's Eve, the feeling inside prison changed. The sense of introspection that happens on ordinary days is there, the feel of the weight of time on everyone. I felt my loneliness surface as I thought about how others on the outside were enjoying the freedom of fully partaking in the magic of holiday spirit. Those were some of the toughest times for me, times when I felt the weight of time, times when I wished I could grow wings and fly home.

> The Christmas dinner was pretty good: roasted chicken leg, a slice of roast beef, wax green beans, roasted potatoes, brown gravy, two slices of wheat bread, and green salad (with pieces of tomatoes!), and Italian dressing in a squeeze packet. For dessert we received individually wrapped double-crusted pumpkin pie. We also got an extra 2 minutes to eat.
>
> —*Letter from Wasco to a friend, December 25, 2003*

I tried to spend most of my time inside staying busy since downtime led to daydreaming, and unless an inmate is short (time to the streets under six months), daydreams were seeds for depression. I drew much from books such as *Man's Search for Meaning*, by Viktor Frankl, MD. Drawing from his dreadful concentration camp experience, Frankl captured what I discovered myself in a far less desperate imprisonment, that "everything can be taken from man but one thing: the last of human freedoms—to choose one's attitude in any given set of circumstances, to choose one's own way."[5] This philosophy of self–mental determination, by choice, was then and remains a key lesson I draw upon in my life.

The DOM: Counts and Recounts

Prison officials are paranoid. They have to be. Real danger comes with the job. Walk through a haunted house on Halloween and you expect something to jump out and scare the crap out of you. Prison staff— guards, medical staff, administrators, and contracted laborers—work in an environment that can become hostile in a blink, any time, any day. Prison staff are closely knit and work in potential combat zones watching for signs of imminent insurrection. The mixture of diagnosable human personality disorders squeezed together in prisons is vast, and the grand mixing and storing of human beings experiencing incessant fears and anxiety and feelings of unrequited hatred toward others, and those embedded in gang cultures make the efficient and safe management of a prison no mean task. Staff's welfare is grounded in accounting for every inmate at every moment. Of course, this is impossible, but the CDCR's Department of Operations Manual is called *the DOM* by both inmates and staff, and is the guide—the rule book—by which inmates' lives are run.[6] The DOM is where the responsibility for the count is codified: make sure everyone contained is counted. This is known as *count time*, and it happened five times a day, every day, even during sleeping hours. Every one of California's inmates is counted separately, one at a time, every day. Inmates in the infirmary are counted, and all inmate labor report back to their cells or dorms for count. Every empty bunk must have a legitimate reason for being empty. On days I was off the yard, to attend meetings with the warden's representatives, an audit trail of my whereabouts was programmed into the prison *daily*—a computer readout that pinpoints every inmate in the system, leaving a GPS-like paper trail of movement.

At count time the entire yard was recalled. Inmates returned to their bunks. Those in transit, between facilities, or at a local hospital for treatment were counted in absentia. A damped-down hush came over the prison at count, like a charging beast slowing to a trot, yet still burning with fury. Morning count determined whether everyone had returned from breakfast. Meanwhile, the guards in the commissary where inmate labor prepared meals were counting cooking utensils (though inmates don't use knives, not even plastic ones). All yards in the prison were shut down for counts. At Ironwood, where the population hovered around seven thousand, all inmates were locked down simultaneously. There were no bathroom privileges during count.

If you were in a cell during count, you were locked in with your cellmate. If you were in a dorm, the front and only door was locked. Inmates were required to be on their beds for count. Guards did body counts and took a tally. There's supposed to be no talking during count; all electronics are to be turned off. In actuality, there's a buzz in the dorm about blowing the count and being a badass motherfucker who blew the joint. Radios were turned down but not off. The televisions, under the control of the guards, went into a techno-hibernation—a moment that always felt like velvet to my ears since the sound of the televisions drove me crazy. I developed a television phobia in prison, in fact, and have not owned a television since transitioning back to the streets—one thing good I gained from being "down." When I was inside, sleeping with earplugs became my required routine, though I sometimes wondered if I had compromised my safety by plugging my ears while sleeping. After all, inmates were attacked in their sleep, sometimes without known provocation. But I decided to go for the sleep.

During counts I wrote letters, read, or took a nap. If the entire prison tally is off by one inmate, the system locks up. No one leaves where they are; all transportation into or especially leaving the prison immediately stops. Trucks leaving the prison compound are thoroughly searched for stowaway escapees—guards even check under the hood. Teams of guards rush to the surrounding public roadways looking for escapees in the brush or hitchhiking. Helicopters spring from nowhere. Guards, who usually only carry batons, now are armed with guns and rifles that make them look silly but serious. There are few actual escapes or attempts to throw off a count. The main reason for an off count is miscounting bodies.

During the hours it may take to complete a recount, bathroom privileges in the dorm are limited to two or three men at a time. Going to a water fountain is limited in the same way. If the lockdown gets into chow time, the chow is brought to the cells and dorms. It was a neat change to walk in designated rows to pick up a tray, while under guard, and walk back to my bunk and eat. It doesn't take much to break the monotony of daily routines.

Sex

> I have boxed up all my belongings and put them in Mom and Dad's attic. I have packed up my libido, too, and put it in a box marked "open me first."
>
> —*Letter to my sister, October 2003*

Before I went to prison, I had heard the stories about sex inside. I heard the late-night show pundits' voyeuristic and flippant surmises, jokes like the one I heard the morning Jared Fogel, Subway's spokesman, pled guilty to federal child molestation charges. The front page of the *New York Post* read "Enjoy a Foot Long in Jail."[7] I'd heard all the scary stories about rape, gang rapes, and being made the bitch to a drooling character who thereby owned you. In my experience in prison, none of these stories proved true. It's naïve to believe that consensual and nonconsensual sex doesn't happen in prison, and naturally I heard the inferences and conversational conjectures that some guys had something going on sexually. Still, the strong stigma against same-sex relations caused a yard-wide cognitive dissonance.

I do not mean to dismiss the seriousness of same-sex rape in prison; I am saying only that I knew of no such incidents. Rape in prison is serious and recognized by the federal government. In 2001, Human Rights Watch published a comprehensive report called "No Escape," that documented the prevalence and devastating impact of male rape in US prisons. The report resulted in the enactment of Public Law 108-79, known as the 2003 Prison Rape Elimination Act, designed to eliminate inmate-on-inmate and staff-on-inmate sexual violence.[8] But during my time, I noticed more that inmates were generally homophobic, and for the most part, misogynistic. As a result of this mix of extreme perspectives, at times inmates appeared to be full of awkwardness and outright fear. On the yard, the machismo male prevailed; might was right and could save your life. Under Governor Pete Wilson, in February 1998, California prisons banned weights, a ban that ironically continued under the governorship of Arnold Schwarzenegger and on into Governor Jerry Brown's tenure.[9] Still, stationary equipment, bars and sit-up stations in the yards provided an opportunity to tone up and build up.

Of course, there were gay and bisexual men in prison. Some were open about their sexuality, though in being so they were at risk from frightened machismo males who appeared to be subtly intimidated by homosexuality. Since there were not large numbers of openly gay men in any yard I lived in, they were marginalized and as a result had perfected their survival skills. In my prison travels, I felt a sort of kinship to the gay men I met. Being Jewish, having been an attorney, being old enough to be the father of the great majority of men I interacted with, I had my own set of social hurdles to overcome to survive. Like the gay men I met, I was in many ways an outcast in prison.

In the Orange County Jail, openly gay men were made to wear pink jumpsuits to distinguish them from straight men who were issued orange jumpsuits. I never did learn the origin of this rule, only that it existed. Gay men were kept in segregated housing and not mainstreamed into the general jail population. Because their sexuality might become an excuse for physical torment and even murder, they were held in protective custody, though when shipped from jail to prison they were mainstreamed unless they requested protective custody. Few asked for this designation since being in protective custody normally put one in the position of being perceived as weak, or worse, a rat. Prison culture could be maddening, a stew of anger and discomfort and prejudice leading men to lie in wait for prey. Sexual offenses such as child molestation or rape were not tolerated by "regular inmates," but a gay man doing time for a drug offense was considered a sexual offender because of his sexual preference.

One day in May 2004, I happened to have the day off from my library work, so I went to the sally port to check out the bus full of new fish that had just arrived on the yard. One guy stood out—a honey-colored black man named Copp'r had just arrived, loud and flamboyant. As the new arrivals stood in the sally port while their belongings were searched for contraband, Copp'r's voice rose above the other voices. Generally, guards did not perform body-cavity searches—just "bend 'em and spread 'em" followed by "stand up and lift your sack." Uncircumcised men were told to pull back their foreskins (being Jewish does have its advantages). And over time, since this occurs every time an inmate is transported, leaves the yard for medical attention, or has a visit, these indignities became routine.

But that day when Copp'r arrived, I was standing in the sally port because one of my jobs was to provide the new fish orientation about the yard. When Copp'r was told to bend over and spread, he smiled at the inspecting guard and quipped, "Now honey, if you want into my honey spot, you're gonna have to wine and dine me first." The hoots and hollers from those inmates in earshot rapidly turned to subtle fear mixed with machismo disbelief. The guard snapped, "Shut the fuck up and spread 'em wide," and the other inmates, stifling smirks and giggles, moved quickly away from Copp'r.

As part of my job, I also gave out preassigned housing and bunk assignments to the new arrivals. Copp'r turned out to be assigned to a bunk directly across from mine. He and I would sleep feet to feet, a three-foot aisle called *the street* separating our bunks. As I watched the others moving away, I thought this was going to be interesting. Copp'r had a strong personality, different from the mainstream inmates, and I was fairly certain the combination was going to lead to fireworks down the line.

Copp'r was long and lean with the legs of a catwalk model, and he knew it. That evening I watched Copp'r standing by his bunk putting on eye makeup as he was getting ready for chow. He drew eyeliner across his lids and penciled in his brows. He turned and looked at me and asked how his eyebrows looked. For a moment I was stumped. I'd never had a man ask me such a question. "They look okay," I said, because they did. From the start I recognized Copp'r as a flamboyant anomaly and a source of mesmerizing entertainment. Even those men with tattoos plastered thickly on their bodies—some reading "White Power" and "Trust No Bitch"—stood around Copp'r's bunk as he bumped and ground out a lap dance to pulsating and rhythmic tunes. Soon the neighborhood around my bunk became crowded with sex-starved men. Rico, Rock, Spike the Skinhead, and Big Show joined the crowd that was becoming hypnotized by Copp'r's snakelike movements. I think they were making believe, just as I was, that the gyrating body before them was a woman.

Initially the others accepted Copp'r. He was a character with a disarming personality coupled with a black belt in karate—or at least so he said. He may not have had a black belt, but watching him roll his state-issued shorts all the way up to his crotch was mesmerizing, and when he walked around the track on the yard, I envisioned him as a graceful giraffe. And for a while things were quiet.

Copp'r was black, and he and I got along fine. I treated him with respect, as I did all the others. But as time passed, I became wary of the rapidly changing climate toward him. He had effeminate ways of talking, walking, and reacting to controversy. When he was moved from a lower, more preferable bunk to an upper bunk with an "other" inmate, he took issue. He wasn't concerned about what race he bunked with, but he felt he was being disrespected by being moved to a top bunk. The longer the time on the yard, the greater likelihood of being switched to a lower bunk, and only a doctor's note trumps the shot callers' bunk assignments, but now a white shot caller was moving Copp'r against his will, and he complained.

The whites wanted Copp'r to just get over it. The blacks, temporarily forgetting about Copp'r's sexuality, thought the white shot caller had acted with prejudice against Copp'r. Tensions mounted until one day I made the mistake of walking the track around the yard with Copp'r to try to give him a sense of the racial stirrings his complaint was creating. My mistake was forgetting that he was black and that whites and blacks never walked the yard together, nor did they mix during leisure time, television time, chow time, sports time, exercise time, or when it came to sharing anything. When Copp'r had first walked on the yard he was interesting and funny, but by now he had become a target, and once that happened, the other inmates focused on his homosexuality. No longer was he considered funny, no longer entertainment. Instead he was a troublemaker, and in prison being different usually fed into the generalized paranoia; if you're not understood, you're a threat. Fear coupled with paranoia launched the beginning of catcalls and sometimes escalated to fistfights or stabbings.

Over time I'd become acutely conscious of how the culture of prison worked when it came to homosexuality. Gay men who kept a low profile and performed domestic functions were not perceived as threatening. Gays who altered clothes or had other sewing skills were welcome additions to the yard population. Generally, gay men avoided situations that led to confrontations, but more than two gay men on the yard together, in conversation or just walking the track, could spike paranoia and false rumors about what they might be planning. As a rule, prison demanded straight men never be seen showering with someone who was known as gay. Most prison shower facilities provided space for up to five men to shower at one time, but as one white car key holder said to me early on, "It just doesn't look right." If a straight man were seen showering with a gay man, rumors of illicit sex quickly telegraphed around the yard. And Copp'r had overstepped all bounds.

Indeed, showers often set the stage for sexual comments, especially if anyone bent over to pick up a dropped bar of soap, usually eliciting snide remarks about angles and sodomy. A second drop of a soap bar would find you in an empty shower. I carried my bar of soap in a sock and attached a piece of string through the open end so that I could hang the soap in a sock on a faucet, allowing for efficient lathering with no chance of dropping the bar.

At the same time, in prison, one of the most common pastimes was masturbation. Sexual energy and desire do not abate in prison—especially since there is no access to women. Pornography that does not expose female or male frontal genital nudity was allowed, but there was also often an unmarked manila envelope that circulated around, a manila envelope with lurid magazines displaying serious female genital nudity. I never knew how these pictures got on the yard—perhaps through the mail or via the guards. And some yards had a *jack shack*, the designated shower where inmates were able to shower and masturbate while surrounded by nude pictures preserved in sheets of plastic. Jack shacks were private, allowing just one inmate at a time, and whoever used it, cleaned it. Another favorite masturbatory convenience was the old athletic sock lubricated with Vaseline. Called *pleasure purses*, these were not sanctioned by the state, which made getting caught red-handed in the act a punishable offense. As a result, masturbation went underground, undercover. After all, there is seldom any stopping healthy, confined men from engaging in unilateral, sexual release.

California Penal Code Section 311 says that representations of persons engaged in sexual acts, actual or simulated, masturbation, excretory functions or lewd exhibitions of genitals are obscene,[10] and mail, incoming and outgoing, is screened for such content. What inmates write about to others was of interest to the prison administration. Authorities read the mail, focusing on escapes, drug trafficking, plans for physical attacks on inmates, former inmates and crime victims and witnesses, hate mail, criminal networking, and clues about anything unlawful happening or being planned within the prison. They also focused on pornography since obscenity is not permitted under the law.[11]

On the yard, pornography is further defined as the presentation of sexually arousing material in literature, art, motion pictures, or other means of communication or expression. That included adult frontal genital nudity of either sex. As a result, lockers and flat surfaces around bunks were often plastered with topless women with come-hither grins, but only female guards and female sergeants strictly enforced the rules against such postings. Female guards had a relatively unobstructed view of bathroom facilities and showers so that any modicum of modesty was lost to the inmate. And of course, restrictions on pornographic materials, like prohibitions on drugs and cigarette smoking, only made their circulation a source for underground exploitation. As with other contraband, there was a prison underground. Put five hundred men on a yard with nothing but time to watch and study rules imposed by the administration and they will find cracks in those routines, opportunities for spreading messages, photographs, drugs, and cell phones. Like other secretive communication systems, creativity, human ingenuity, raw intelligence, and an element of risk fueled the underground. Risk was usually shrugged off with a laugh, "What are they going to do if they catch me, put me in prison?" And so, if anyone wanted to borrow a folder of all-inclusive pornographic material (always heterosexual), the cost was a bag of chips for thirty minutes or a box of macaroni and cheese for an hour. And the borrower had to return the exact number of photos being leased, with no pages stuck together.

The rule makers' perspective of inmates' sexual conduct was conflicted by their own regulations and laws. The regulations and laws conflicted with recognized trends about the transmission of HIV/AIDS in the prisons. The code of regulation, in California, left little ambiguity about what its intentions were with regard to sexual conduct between inmates. California law is clear: all sex acts, including consensual, between inmates are prohibited by California Code of Regulations Title 15, Section 3007. Like other Title 15 regulations, they are prescribed by the director of the correctional department as part of the administration of the prisons. Section 3007 provides "Inmates may not participate in illegal sexual acts. Inmates are specifically excluded in laws which remove legal restraints from acts between consenting adults. Inmates must avoid deliberately placing themselves in situations and behaving in a manner which is designed to encourage illegal sexual acts."[12]

While California lawmakers were aware that HIV/AIDS was a concern within the state's penal system, California Penal Code Section 7500 could not be clearer: "(b) The spread of AIDS and hepatitis B and C within prison and jail populations presents a grave danger to inmates within those populations, law enforcement personnel, and other persons in contact with a prisoner infected with the AIDS virus, both during and after the prisoner's confinement."[13]

But in October 2007, when Governor Arnold Schwarzenegger was presented with a bill to provide condoms to inmates, the result was political pinball. Supporters of the bill pointed to compelling statistics in their lobbying efforts to get passage. For example, the Correctional HIV Consortium's estimated annual cost of care for an HIV-positive inmate was $80,396.[14] In 2004, AB1677, Nursing Education: Service in Public Hospitals and Veterans' Facilities, was introduced in the California state assembly, in part to require that the director of corrections allow any nonprofit or public health care agency to distribute sexual barrier protection devices such as condoms and dental dams.[15] On November 30, 2004, the portion of the bill pertaining to condoms being issued in prison was deleted without further action.

People opposed the condom/sexual barrier protection bill and the governor vetoed the bill because it conflicted with state law that made sexual contact among inmates illegal. While the governor did acknowledge that condom distribution represented a reasonable "public policy, and it is consistent with the need to improve our prison health care system and overall public health," he lacked the political courage to do the right thing for inmates and others with whom inmates would engage in sexual activity upon release.

The governor's veto ruled, and the bill failed despite persuasive and apolitical points offered by proponents of the bill such as the inmate condom programs in place in Vermont, Mississippi, Canada, Australia, and most of the European Union. Within jail systems, proponents pointed to the New York City, Washington, DC, San Francisco, and Los Angeles systems, which have condom distribution programs in operation. That made no difference.

The broad application of sexual repression impacts all inmates. The hardest hit group, however, were the younger men facing double-digit sentences, and those, young and older, serving life sentences. The number of inmates serving life sentences under California's three-strikes-and-you're-out sentencing rules swelled the ranks of inmates directly resulting in the excessive crowding of the California's thirty-three men's prisons. Under certain circumstances in California, conjugal visits were allowed between husband and wife, but California inmates were not screened for HIV/AIDS. Every time they entered the prison system or were transferred from one facility to another, inmates were tested for TB, but an inmate's HIV/AIDS status remained a secret and a problem for many.

All inmates struggle with restrictions and madness and confinement and prejudice and political pinball. People like Copp'r suffer, but so does everyone else. I learned my lesson that day on the yard when Copp'r and I were walking together. I couldn't break any prison rules—written or not, spoken or unspoken. I would learn that Copp'r was eventually beaten severely by inmates who would no longer tolerate him—a fate that haunts me still.

Cruel and Unusual Punishment

In our culture the phrase "cruel and unusual punishment" is well known. We learn it in American history classes when we're first taught about our

Constitution. The phrase is in the Bill of Rights, the first ten amendments to the Constitution, ratified in 1791. The Eighth Amendment contains the phrase in one sentence: "Excessive bail shall not be required, nor excessive fines imposed, nor cruel and unusual punishments inflicted."

Combining the words *cruel* and *unusual* to describe a punishment provides fertile ground for debate about precisely when a situation or condition satisfies the combined meanings. Simply put, the Bill of Rights phrase is intended to prohibit penalties being imposed in a barbaric, excessive, and bizarre manner by the government. Since 1791, the term *cruel and unusual* has been affirmatively used to prohibit acts of punishment such as disemboweling alive, burning at the stake, crucifying, beheading, breaking on a wheel, and drawing and quartering. But over the decades as our society progressed in regard to human rights and the enactment of penalties by the states and the federal government, the amendment has continually been reinterpreted to fit with the social mores of the times. In 1958, the Supreme Court ruled that "the Eighth Amendment must draw its meaning from the evolving standards of the decency that mark the progress of a maturing society."[16]

In 1972, Justice William Brennan wrote in a majority opinion: "There are, then, four principles by which we may determine whether a particular punishment is 'cruel and unusual.' . . . A punishment must not, by its severity, be degrading to human dignity," especially torture. "A severe punishment that is obviously inflicted in wholly arbitrary fashion. A severe punishment that is clearly and totally rejected throughout society. A severe punishment that is patently unnecessary."[17]

In the 1990s, the Supreme Court broadened the interpretation of *cruel and unusual* to mean, in more humanistic terms, that the use of excessive physical force against a prisoner may rise to the level of cruel and unusual punishment even if the inmate does not suffer serious injury.[18]

During my prison term, I encountered one particular situation I felt violated the "cruel and unusual" clause, but I could do little about it. No one with authority cared about the overcrowded living conditions in the dorms, the two-man cells, the mess hall, or the bathrooms.

For instance, something very wrong took place in the Orange County Jail on that day in August 2004 when the guards took it upon themselves to cram one hundred ten of us into a room meant for thirty-five and then turned off the air. I was sure some of us would die. I'm certain the Orange County sheriff's actions in this instance would qualify as cruel and unusual under Justice Brennan's definition. The essential predicate of degrading human dignity premised by racist motivations was apparent and acted upon in a wholly arbitrary fashion upon the whim of a demented power-gorged individual and his cronies. The cruelty of the conduct was patently unnecessary to those of us who posed no threat or danger to anyone. Nearly everyone would find the behavior cruel and unusual—at least so I believe. Years after I had served my term, I came upon a play by Tennessee Williams that reawakened the memories and feelings associated with that Orange County Jail incident. *Not about Nightingales,* written in 1938, was inspired by what newspaper reports called the "Klondike" atrocity that happened in a Pennsylvania prison. An October 11, 1938 *Look* magazine article on the subject gave this account:

> One day late in August, 650 inmates of the Philadelphia County prison in Holmesberg, PA, struck against a monotonous diet of hamburger and spaghetti, refused their supper. Three days later the naked, tortured bodies of four prisoners were found in an airtight cell. They had been scalded to death.

> An investigation was launched. Prison guards and officers were arrested. The American public was shocked to learn that "hot steam treatment" had been given to twenty-five unruly prisoners. A cry for "justice" arose. But there is scant justice in most American prisons, and county jails are generally worst of the lot.

Medical Care at Ironwood—Cruel and Unusual

After I had settled into my daily routine at Ironwood, I began to take an interest in the operations of E-Yard and the prison as a whole. Morris Teitlebaum and I were elected to be the Men's Advisory Council (MAC) yard president and secretary, respectively. No one else ran for office. As MAC officers, we represented the inmates on E-Yard on issues related to living conditions, suggestions for improvements in food and services, and for expressing general gripes and grievances associated with living on the yard. He and I were transported once a month to the main administration building housed on the D-Yard to meet with the warden or the warden's lieutenants. We took our roles seriously, and doing our jobs was a wonderful distraction from the mundane routines of life on the yard.

Ironwood is a sprawling compilation of five separate yards—A through E. I quickly discovered that the most serious problem on the yard was the acute failure to meet the medical needs of many inmates. Reports of delayed treatment came to Morris and me, and we began keeping a detailed log of responses to medical emergencies that lagged and were delayed, resulting in exacerbated conditions due to a lack of competent medical staff or poor or nonexistent communications between the yard, Central Health, and the prison's hospital on D-Yard. These problems were compounded by a systemic malaise toward attention to critical needs. Ultimately Morris and I determined that the root problem was the lack of a workable triage system to assign degrees of urgency to injuries and illnesses and to decide the order of treatment when there were large numbers of medical situations.

We reported the situation to Assistant Warden Flamer on November 15, 2004, during a MAC meeting. The assistant warden welcomed our concerns and asked for details, in writing, so he could investigate each situation and generate his own report to the warden. After working through the night on the project, Michael and I placed our November 16, 2004 report in the prison mail addressed to the assistant warden and signed by both of us. Below are verbatim highlights of that report:

Re: Follow-Up to November 15, 2004, Meeting

Per your request, I am providing a sampling of delayed medical care scenarios indicative of poor triage procedures on E-Yard.

Attached to this memo are written statements, by each inmate, which provide firsthand details of their experiences.

Each inmate has given his consent for me to convey their medical information. They have further given consent for you to utilize their information, within CDC, in furtherance of its evaluation of the delayed medical program on this yard.

Robert Doe, CDC Kxxx (actual names and CDC numbers are not used for privacy purposes).

This was followed by a detailed list of individuals' medical issues secondary to poor medical intervention and care.

Brown v. Plata

In April 2001, the Prison Law Office in Berkeley, California, filed a class-action lawsuit on behalf of Marciano Plata and other prisoners, charging that California prisons were in violation of the ban against cruel and unusual punishment as provided by the Eighth Amendment.[19] The suit relied heavily on the live testimony of experts and representatives of state agencies, and reports of experts in the fields of medicine, psychiatry, and prison administration.

The issue the Supreme Court was considering in the *Plata* case was this: does a court order requiring California to reduce its prison population to remedy unconstitutional conditions in its prisons violate existing law?

On May 23, 2011, in a five-to-four decision, Justice Anthony Kennedy's majority ruling wielded a thunderous indictment of the conditions in which inmates suffered as charges of the California prison system.[20] The decision upheld a federal appellate court's decision by a panel of three judges that serious overcrowding in California's thirty-three prisons was the "primary cause" for violations of the Eighth Amendment.[21]

Justice Kennedy wrote that "the court-mandated population limit is necessary to remedy the violation of prisoners' constitutional rights and is authorized by [law]."

The next effect of the *Plata* decision was an order to release enough prisoners, over time, so the California inmate population would come within 137.5 percent of the prisons' total design capacity. That amounted to releasing between thirty-eight thousand and forty-six thousand inmates. The state was ordered to comply with the reduction "without delay."

Following are examples of the deficiencies cited in Justice Kennedy's opinion:

1. Inadequate medical screening of incoming prisoners.

2. Delays in or failure to provide access to medical care, including specialist care.

3. Untimely responses to medical emergencies.

4. The interference of custodial staff with the provision of medical care.

5. The failure to recruit and retain sufficient numbers of competent medical staff.

6. Disorganized and incomplete medical records.

7. A lack of quality control procedures, including lack of physician peer review, quality assurance, and death reviews.

8. A lack of protocols to deal with chronic illnesses, including diabetes, heart disease, hepatitis, and HIV.

9. The failure of the administrative grievance system to provide timely or adequate responses to complaints concerning medical care.

The claims alleged that patients being treated by the CDCR received inadequate medical care that resulted in the deaths of thirty-four inmate-patients.

Justice Kennedy described egregious conditions found by experts who visited California prisons as fact finders for the panel of federal judges:

1. Suicidal patients were being held in "telephone-booth sized cages without toilets" for prolonged periods of time because there was simply no other place to hold them.[22]

2. One correctional officer testified that as many as fifty sick prisoners could be held in a twelve-by-twenty-foot cage for up to five hours while they waited for medical treatment.

3. One report found wait times for mental-health care as long as twelve months.

4. Another analysis estimated sixty-eight preventable suicides or possibly preventable suicides due to failure to provide psychiatric care.

5. "The degree of overcrowding in California's prisons is exceptional. California's prisons are designed to house a population just under 80,000, but . . . the population was almost double that."[23]

6. The State's prisons had operated at around 200 percent of design capacity for at least eleven years.

7. "Prisoners are crammed into spaces neither designed nor intended to house inmates."[24]

8. Inadequate mental health care. "A psychiatric expert reported observing an inmate who had been held in such a cage for nearly

24 hours, standing in a pool of his own urine, unresponsive and nearly catatonic."[25]

9. Defficient medical treatment. There were 557 preventable deaths in a one-year period. The relied-upon report found that a preventable death occurred every six to seven days in the California prison system.

The oral argument held before the Supreme Court in the *Plata* case contains insights into how the Supreme Court justices weighed on the issue before the Court. The Appellant, the State of California, was represented by Carter G. Phillips, Esq., and the Appellees—the class action plaintiffs in addition to Mr. Plata—were represented by Donald Spector.

Following are transcript excerpts from the November 30, 2010, oral argument:[26]

Justice Sonia Sotomayor: Well, the best interest of the State of California, isn't it to deliver adequate constitutional care to the people that it incarcerates?

That's a constitutional obligation.

Mr. Phillips: Absolutely! And California recognizes that.

Justice Sonia Sotomayor: So when are you going to get to that?

When are you going to avoid the needless deaths that were reported in this record?

When are you going to avoid or get around people sitting in their feces for days in a dazed state?

When are you going to get to a point where you are going to deliver care that is going to be adequate? . . .

Justice Anthony M. Kennedy: And—and—and just if I can have your attention for a moment, I have this problem with the case. Overcrowding is of course always the cause. If I am running a hotel—if I am looking at a highway system, I need a highway, what's the number of cars? If the problem is bad service in a hotel, well, it's the number of employees per—per guest.

I mean, that's fairly simple. . . .

Mr. Phillips: I mean, again, one of the real flaws in this case, Justice Kennedy, is nobody doubts for a moment that there have been very significant violations of constitutional rights years gone by, and indeed a failure on the mental health side ultimately to get you—get to the point where we are in fact providing a significant remedy.

The *Plata* decision ruled that California must stop imprisoning so many people and that the state must take steps to reduce the state's prison population by thirty-three thousand. The decision led to California's historic realignment process that continues today.[27] The intent of the realignment process is to help the state reverse decades of over-reliance upon incarceration. The success of the realignment program is subject to debate and beyond the scope of this book.

CHAPTER SIX

The Rules of
the Game

Witnessed strange, pathological behavior around lunchtime. Both televisions blaring the same story on the same Los Angeles news station
KABC-television. Commercial airline tracked by air escorts. Landing
gear stuck in well of plane. 50 or so onboard. Press built it up for sure
disaster. Big crunch to get a good view. Some guys cheer for crash—
sounds like football game. Plane made successful landing, sparks and
smoke—some guys yelling "blow up, burn mutha-fucker." Much disappointment, back to boredom . . . dumfounded.

—*Journal entry, May 11, 2005*

T HE NATURE OF COMMUNICATIONS in prison is broad—
covering different genres that include television, letter writing,
phone calls, packages, contracts to kill or maim (kites), colors,
sign language, horseplay, CDCR forms, and tattoos. Whatever the form
of communication, anything that breaks the relentless boredom of incarceration helps remind inmates that they are connected to outside civiliza-
tion. After only a few weeks of being programmed to a daily routine,
a hollowness spawned by boredom and loneliness settles in your gut.
There's little within the prison environment to stimulate the mind—no
primary colors—so my memories come in sepia, noisy sepia, because in
prison there is never silence. Never.

Television is the babysitter of the masses in prison. Day rooms have immoveable television benches segregated by race. Blacks and others decide programming on one side, whites and Mexicans on the other. These independent rights included news, sports, and talk shows. One side watched Oprah, while the other side preferred Maury. You're wrong if you thought it was the blacks who watched the *Oprah Winfrey Show*. Nothing is more real in prison than the surreal.

Some television programming united the masses more than sports, talk shows, and unpredictable news reports could. This was the Los Angeles car chases. These brought everyone together for careful, concentrated viewing. The excitement of the chase and the knowledge that people could get hurt and that the cops always won produced roars of delight whenever the chased driver with his blood-chilling, out-of-control flee-or-die hormones raging outmaneuvered authorities. When the chased got caught, wrestled to the ground, and cuffed, the overriding critique was what a dumb fuck the chased guy had been.

At Ironwood, other inmates spent hours finding and bonding with local desert critters. Scorpions are ubiquitous in the Sonoran Desert, scuttling around inside and outside the prison's perimeter. They sneak under rocks and dive into crevices in cement, asphalt, and rocks. They also gravitate to shoes, boots, and underwear. Early in my time at Ironwood, I learned a lesson about desert living: always check your shoes and shorts before putting them on. I won't forget the crunch and ooze after slipping my bare foot into a hard leather shoe. The guys around me laughed without empathy. I hosed the shoe for twenty minutes and dried it in the scorching sun on the aluminum bleachers by the softball field; the shoe shrank from size 8 to size 6, so I got rid of it.

After that, for several weeks, I looked out of the long, narrow window of a two-man cell gazing into nothing. One day I saw a green weed that had popped out of a crack in the asphalt separating my housing unit from the one just a few feet away. The weed was able to live under the hot sun because it spent more than half of its day in shade in the narrow alley between the buildings. After a week, the weed sported a bright yellow flower, and two weeks later, during a blustery sandstorm, nature blew the weed away, and with it our communion flew away too.

In general, staying in contact with family, friends, and local news is important to most inmates—it's important to be reminded that one is human, loved, and remembered. Friends and family and their kindness and love fill the void left by the system's messages of inadequacy, insignificance, irrelevance, and unworthiness. Communication with those loved ones for me and others I knew helped counteract the loneliness and boredom, bringing organization to the internal chaos. Because life inside is so monotonous, I discovered that real feeling lived within the changes in the daily program.

Monotony and predictability, day after day, wear down the defenses to prison-bred stagnation and cause agitation, sadness, anger, remorse, risk taking, and flights of wild imagination. Prison unrest is deeply seated in boredom. Men (and women and juveniles, too) with time to kill will find simple and creative ways to make life more exciting, regardless of the risk. Matters of little significance become magnified and potentially explosive as clocks tick slowly and calendars flip pages at a snail's pace.

The manufacturing of pruno was one example of a break from the boredom. The thrill of the cat-and-mouse game (would the coppers find it?) broke the routine. Other thrills drove otherwise rational men to perform irrational acts. In the manufacturing of pruno, inmates experienced a thrill three times: first in the thrill of manufacturing, then in the risk of getting caught and being punished, and third in the thrill of the Friday-night buzz that seeped into Sunday. I was never sure if the buzz was so desirable because getting drunk reminded men of their lives on the street or if it was more important to self-medicate, to achieve numbness—or if there was no real difference between the two.

Once, outside the dorm and to the left around the side toward the back in a spot where the building's edge was just out of direct sight of the CO's office, someone offered me a puff of marijuana. I had lost sight of the risk. I was driven to take a puff. I knew it was wrong. My level-headed mind unpersuasively mumbled, *Get yourself together, man,* but that rational mind was too weak to influence the desire. For a couple of hours after that, I faked being high, a pleasant diversion from the dullness of routine.

The Zimbardo Experiment

My knowingly using pot on the yard was not something I would have predicted about myself, but in that moment, my thoughtful, balanced approach to doing my time vanished in the blink of an eye. The risk of being caught and thus tacking up to six more months to my sentence were sidelined. Why? The only way I can make any sense of this is in thinking about the Stanford Prison Experiment (SPE), a 1971 experiment conceived of and conducted by Professor Philip Zimbardo at Stanford. Reading the study, I found the answer to my potentially self-destructive behavior and temporary transformation of character.

The SPE created what Dr. Zimbardo labeled *situational power*. The mock prison created in the basement of the psychology building on the Stanford University campus was hardly a prison like Ironwood State Prison, but the environment created for the experiment evoked an authentic transformation of personalities. Some fake "guards" took on the personalities of real guards, and fake "inmates" exhibited psychological conducts and affects that real inmates, men like myself on the yard at Ironwood that day, experience.

The experiment was scheduled to run fourteen days. Dr. Zimbardo arbitrarily selected twenty-four male college students to be guards and prisoners. Within two days, the personalities of some of the guards changed abruptly. They became verbally, physically, and emotionally abusive to the prisoners. Dr. Zimbardo created the functional equivalent of a jail or prison environment that enabled authentic recreation of the experience of losing one's personal identity, caused, in great part, by arbitrary, sustained, and continuous control of inmates' behavior plus the deprivation of privacy. In trying to understand my decision to take a puff of marijuana and risk severe punishment, some lessons from the SPE were helpful.

The first of ten lessons identified by Dr. Zimbardo was that "some situations can exert powerful influences over individuals, causing them to behave in ways they would not, could not, predict in advance. . . . In trying to understand the causes of complex, puzzling behavior, it is best to start with a situational analysis"[1] Dr. Zimbardo's explanation of situational power, the second lesson from the SPE, also gave me insight into why I used pot that day. Situational power is most salient in novel settings in which the participants cannot call on previous guidelines for their new behavior and have no historical references to rely on and in which their habitual ways of behaving and coping are not reinforced.[2]

My momentary internal rationale for smoking pot had shades of both lessons. The constant situational, institutionalized boredom of prison life put me on the lookout for a high, a thrill, and I took it. Under my particular circumstances, and although I deliberately stayed strong in my mind, I could not have predicted my own change in personality at the instant I consented. This is not an excuse for my conduct. If I had been caught, I would not have had a convincing or acceptable defense. I was bored, and I was lonely. I acted to quell these heavy feelings.

Free Expression

> Notice of poetry/original writing. Starting on June 13, 2004, 7:00 PM under the northwest tree by Program. All are encouraged to come recite one or more of your original writings // or just enjoy and appreciate the beauty of words & the composition of Art. For more details . . . see Mark the A.M. Clerk in the Facility Library, and/or see me, Copp'r.

> —*Flyer circulated by Copp'r for a program he and I tried to create*

Inmates often found their own way of expressing feelings, usually done privately. I discovered over time that some wrote poetry, others wrote music, short stories, essays, or plays. Copp'r and I decided to put together the advertised gathering, and we obtained permission from the yard lieutenant to gather close to the program office where the guards were housed when they were on duty. This was for safety purposes. I was surprised by the remarkable interest generated in the gathering. Men who were otherwise low-key and inexpressive stopped me to show me their original work and to tell me they wanted to participate. It was soothing and healthy for all of us, and I looked forward to the gathering. Unfortunately, a day or two before it was to happen, I was rolled up in the early morning and transported to Orange County to testify as a witness in Melanie Blum's criminal trial. Three months later when I returned, Copp'r was gone. I learned that within days of my departure, he had been severely beaten by a band of inmates who had had enough of his bon vivant homosexual style. I never saw my friend again.

Boredom and loneliness often go together. They are brought on by the repetition of scheduling, such as the five daily head counts, food menus that don't have much variety, always being closely monitored, being on the yard, lock-ins, lockouts, and weekend and holiday blues. Sensory sensations are numbed by such conditions as televisions constantly spewing dumbed-down programming and being told when to sleep and when to wake up. The loss of individuality is a by-product of prison packing machines.

The rules that cause rigidity can also cause harsh realities. An inmate with a terminally ill relative or a close relative who died usually became an inmate rolled up into a single cell lock for an undetermined amount of time. The administrators' rationale was that an inmate suffering such losses is an escape risk and therefore, for the safety of the inmate and for other inmates and staff, he would be segregated from the general population.

As quoted in the beginning of chapter 4, Oscar Wilde, who spent two years in Reading Gaol (jail) for homosexual activities, wrote the words that best describe, for me, the burden of time in jail. His strong sentiment written in his 1898 poem, "Ballad of Reading Gaol" underscores the helplessness the drag of time causes in the prison.

Rules, regulations, and guidelines dictate every aspect of every day of every inmate's life. Whether instituted by the CDCR or dictated by and for inmates, rules impact prison life by prescribing how and when to do the right thing. These restrictions morph in well-honed traditions that dictate decorum and proper etiquette. For example, an unwritten rule of inmate etiquette is to knock on the chow table three times before leaving the table. This is a ritual of respect.

I learned to adapt to the rules of the game very quickly. Being trained and practicing as a lawyer requires this ability to understand and react to legal situations to ensure the best representation of one's clients. Successful trial lawyers must react on their feet quickly in court with nearly instant legal assessments.

Rule 1

Riot on A yard between whites and Mexicans caused a two-hour delay in clearing the afternoon count. Went to chow at 7:20 PM, two hours late. Black and white tensions have washed into our yard; we will be shut down tomorrow.

—*Journal entry, July 15, 2005*

Being trained as a lawyer and then immersed in the legal system, I learned to rapidly evaluate situations for fairness, using common sense and the law. Studying constitutional law cases and applying them to real situations builds a strong foundation to draw upon for identifying right and wrong when peoples' rights are at issue. Over the last century, the United States Supreme Court has set strong guidelines prohibiting discrimination based on age, gender, religion, disability, and race. With regard to the latter, the cases have greatly relaxed the overt and hidden tensions created by society's reinforcement of learned, aberrant interpersonal behaviors.

Growing up in New York in the 1950s and '60s, I recall experiencing remnants of overt racial discrimination and marginalization on family drives to Florida during school vacations. On those trips, I saw the signs and experienced my separation from others because of my skin color. The signs in South Carolina and Georgia, in the sleepy towns where the interstate was not complete, often read White Bathroom or Colored Bathroom, White Drinking Fountain or Colored Drinking Fountain, Tourist Cabins for Negroes, White and Colored Served, and Colored Waiting Line. These signs disturbed me because they didn't seem fair.

In the Westbury Unified School District, I sat in classrooms with children of color, I ate with them in the cafeteria, I played with them on the schoolyard, and we joked and laughed with each other regardless of race. Yes, as a kid I overheard snippets of adult conversations about "block busting" and how a "mixed couple" had moved into a home after the husband, a white man, purchased the house and then brought his black wife and beautiful daughter and son to the neighborhood. The labeling and mistreatment of this family taught me about learned intolerance.

But it was on those long rides to Florida in the family's 1953 Plymouth Cranbrook that my sense of fairness to others was planted and took root. When I saw a sign that directed white or black use of toilet fixtures and water fountains, I assumed my mother would understand this curious designation, and I asked her what it meant. She told me that the signs were wrong and hurtful to black people and that all this would change someday. "It's not right," she would repeat, the look on her face unhappy. She reassured me that the mothers of black children love them just as much as the mothers of white kids love theirs, and no one had the right to deliberately restrict one race from doing what people of other races did. That lesson remained with me and extended to people of every color and creed. Little did I know back then that the lessons from those Florida road trips would serve me well in my life as well as in prison.

I first experienced state-sanctioned racism in the Orange County Jail. After processing through medical and being stripped and searched, I was grouped with other inmates and rapidly put through the showers and issued an orange jail jumpsuit and state-issued flip-flops. During this shifting and sifting check-in process, races were mixed as guards told all of us—no matter our race—to shut up and not ask questions. Our questions, we were told, would be answered along the way, or an experienced inmate would tell us what to expect. When anyone dared complain, the guards would snap, "If you don't like it, don't come to jail." And then came the battery of questions: Any prescription drugs? Gang affiliations? Race? Feel like killing yourself or someone else? This your first rodeo? Any enemies in jail at this time? Any reason to put you in protective custody? The question about religious preference stymied me, but when I asked why I was obliged to state a preference, the guard explained that if I were killed in prison, the Department of Corrections would dispatch the appropriate chaplain to accompany my body to my relatives.

I was processed into the jail system in the late afternoon, and I did not know then that answering Caucasian to the race question meant that I would be housed only with other whites or Hispanics. That was the start of the learning curve about the racial divide in the California penal system—all of which was counterintuitive.

In midyear 2005 when I was serving my time, according to the United States Department of Justice, the California inmate population was 166,532 and the racial divide broke down as follows: Hispanics 37 percent, whites 29 percent, blacks 29 percent, and others 6 percent.[3] The overt segregation I experienced inside opened my eyes and made me feel troubled and dizzy.

When prisoners are awaiting assignment to a cell or dormitory, races are not segregated. In the Orange County Jail we were gathered into small Plexiglas holding cells in what was termed the *loop*. Just writing that word makes me shudder. The loop was a series of cement holding areas with one Plexiglas wall that looked out into the hallway where a dozen or more cells housed other men awaiting bunk assignments. The sign over the door read "Capacity 25," but it was not unusual for thirty-five to forty men of every race to be crammed into these cement boxes, with one rancid stainless-steel toilet bowl, a disgusting stainless steel sink, and a water fountain that often did not work. A continuous cement bench ran around the perimeter of the boxes, and some of them had cement benches in the middle of the box for sitting and sleeping.

In those cells I learned how to find comfort while sleeping on cement with nothing but my clothing as padding. I also learned how to imagine the cement slab was starting to break down, giving way to my weight. I learned that the mind can do wonders, and having an active mind, it turned out, was a gift. My imagination didn't stop with the creature comforts but extended into mind games, a belief that cement is penetrable with the mind and would collapse and dissolve into dust as my cellmates and I walked over the rubble to freedom. Breaking down the molecules and atoms that comprise the cement took a lot of mental time and energy, but in prison time is expendable.

I was in the loop for twenty-four hours, and it was hard being locked down with total loss of free will and creature comforts. The air circulation was near stagnant, and the echoing of the voices in the boxes made me want to scream. There was no peace in the boxes. And there was no racial tension.

The tension started after cell assignments. I was initially housed with five other men, whites and Hispanics. I was quiet, listening to those men more experienced than I who mostly spoke about the days' schedules, watching television in the day room, the food served in the commissary, the canteen that day, moving on to their reception prison, and how ultimately great it would be to arrive at their final prison assignment. I learned there how to detect when the guards were coming around to do a count, and I learned about the enhanced buzzer.

"That's chow time" chirped one of my cellies. Seconds later, the door to our cell popped open simultaneously with the others, and I followed men into a narrow hallway that fronted the doors to each cell. "Follow me," Toad, one of my new cellies, admonished me. Toad stood up against a wall opposite the cell doors where a line was forming behind him. He was the shot caller for my cell, the one with the most experience on navigating the labyrinth of rules, regulations, and indigenous prison culture and on how to stay alive and relatively happy. I began walking to the end of the rapidly forming chow line when Toad asked me where the fuck I was going. "You're white, Roseman; you come with me to the head of the line. whites are always first for chow."

I immediately felt ridiculous.

The chow line racial pecking order was fully entrenched in the Orange County Jail. It looked like this: first in line were whites, behind whites were English-speaking Hispanics, and behind them were the non-English speaking Hispanics. Blacks and others were housed in a separate section of the jail and fed separately. When I realized this, I wondered how this could be, and when I asked, I heard, "If you don't like it, don't come to jail."

From that point forward, I studied the segregation in the California prison system, racial segregation that is sanctioned by the county and state prison systems. I kept a journal on the racial divides. Several of my observations are outlined below.

Food

Upon my arrival at a new prison I sat in the crowded chow hall examining my dinner. Minutes passed before a white inmate walked over to me and said "You're new here, right?" I acknowledged that I was, at which point he told me that I was eating in "their" (black/other) section of the mess hall that I had better move to the other side of the room (where the only seats available were plastic crates along one wall), and that I had better not be seen eating "off bounds" again.

Factory-wrapped and sealed food packages, such as packages of chips or cookies, no matter their original source, are shared openly between whites and Hispanics. Whites, but not Hispanics, can share unopened foodstuffs with blacks, but whites and Hispanics cannot accept unopened edibles from blacks. Food from a chow-hall tray used by a white or Hispanic is never shared with anyone other than another white or Hispanic.

In the dorm at Ironwood I bunked next to Sneakers, a black man. Mixed races were never housed in single-cell situations. I had a top bunk and he had a lower bunk, on the next street (aisle). He had a bad prison cough that kept me up most of the night. I had an opened box of Smith Brothers cough drops, and unaware of the open container restrictions, I offered the opened box to Sneaker while I was sitting on my top bunk and he sat on the lower bunk. "Man, are you crazy? You want to start a race riot? Put that shit away." I took back the box amid the stares of men, some of whom looked scared. If the box had been sealed he would have taken it, but I could not have it back after he opened it.

Another lesson learned: nothing goes unnoticed by other inmates. The cramped conditions and crushing psychology of being locked up in a constant danger zone causes inmates and staff to be survival hypervigilant, and all movement and irregularities are inevitably picked up by others.

Sports

Whites and Hispanics play sports together—softball, handball, volleyball, and horseshoes are strictly segregated. When I asked the white car's holder of the keys about this policy, he told me this separation keeps down potential racial tensions. A black man hits the ball to second base and runs to first—the second baseman throws to first to get the runner out. It's a close call and the white umpire calls the black runner out—ugly racial allegations surface, and the yard flares into a total jumping off (race riot).

Early in my time, I found a softball on the yard close to the playing field. The ball had not been returned to the equipment locker, so I brought it to the locker, which, at the time, was being manned by a black man named Trigger. With others looking, I gave a heads-up to Trigger and threw him the softball. Trigger saw the ball coming but stepped out of its way, and the ball struck a pile of horseshoe rings that plummeted off a shelf and onto the ground. Trigger had stopped a potential racial incident by not catching the ball I threw, and we weren't even playing a game.

Television

On September 3, 2005, the death of Chief Justice William Rehnquist was a lead media story. The usual evening news slot on the white/Hispanic television side was blaring a contemporary dating program, and no one was interested in watching the news. The black/other television was tuned to the news and an in-depth report about Rehnquist was airing. I walked over to the other television and stood under the set while peeking at the screen, trying to hear the report. A black man saw me there, got up from his seat on a bench, and sternly told me that I was creating a stir by my presence. He suggested in a manner that I could not refuse that I move over to my television side or, at least, away from the black/other television.

Sleeping/Housing Arrangements

This rule separates the white/Hispanic (race category A) from the black/other (race category B) races. The A-B designations are my own creation and used only for illustration purposes. Simply put, the rule is A-B inmates cannot share a cell or a double-decker (sometimes triple-decker) bunk. A-A inmates can share living arrangements, and B-Bs can share living arrangements. That's it. There is no such thing as an A-B sleeping and housing arrangement.

I was put into an A-A shared bunk situation in an overcrowded dormitory holding area. My bunkie, Spike was white, but he was also a skinhead. His personal outlook on life was to hate everyone who was not a skinhead, particularly Jews. I felt the tragic irony of the bunk assignment. Spike's head was shaved down to the scalp. The back of his cranium bore a black, rather compelling likeness of the Fuehrer pointing a handgun at anyone approaching from the rear. The left side of his head was inscribed "88," which stood for *Heil Hitler*. The right side of his head revealed a pair of Nazi storm trooper boots. That was not all.

By the time I was released from prison, some two years later, Spike had acquired more tattoos paying homage to the failed Reich. His abdomen was covered with a swastika (swassy); from his shoulders to his lower back was a slender and slinky Eva Braun looking back at the viewer.

Racial matching didn't always prove smart. In the sifting process I had said I was Jewish, but this twenty-six-year-old skinhead had learned to deeply hate Jews. I knew I had to curb my interest in learning more about him. It was tough, but I asked him no questions about his personal beliefs or his ink. When he wrote letters home to his old lady (his girlfriend), he asked me for help with spelling and grammar, so at first we got along just fine.

One hot afternoon I was lying on my top bunk reading *A History of the Jews*.[4] Spike saw the book and became enraged. "You're Jewish . . . I can't bunk with a Jew . . . I need to beat you up . . . What are my comrades going to think? . . . I need to be beat you up" (he repeated this thought). I looked at Spike and watched his light complexion deepen from tomato to eggplant. I told him he would have to request a bunk change because I would not. He got himself moved an hour later, with permission from the white car. How and why I had the guts to stand my ground to a person telling me he had to beat me up is discussed in more detail in chapter 9.

Exercise

Each prison yard has two designated areas for working out, the A and B areas. The pull-up bars, parallel bars, and push-up bars are also strictly restricted by race. When I asked other inmates the reason for the division, I could find no one with any reason other than that's the way it's always been.

Work Assignments

Every prisoner in the system is expected to work. In fact, when I first entered the system, inmates got no half-time credits for good conduct unless they had a work assignment. That policy changed on February 15, 2004. What remains the same is the careful and methodical balancing of races represented by a work group. For example, yard crews comprised of sixteen men were broken down by race, even though the percentage of each race on the yard was not equal. So the crew would be broken down into approximately four individuals from each race.

The reason for the policy, I was told, was to avoid the appearance of a preference for one race over another. Some jobs were more desirable than others. Men obsessed with food wanted to work in the prison kitchen where leftover food and special orders were prepared. Kitchen workers were allowed to take food out of the kitchen, and the extra food was natural barter material for just about anything. Undesirable jobs included work in the warehouse and assignment to cleaning crews given rakes to aimlessly move piles of sand from one location to another in the name of erosion control.

There was one job I wanted—librarian—but the good jobs usually came after the performance of not-so-good jobs. So, after bathroom detail and general porter responsibilities, I was able to get the job I wanted. There were four librarian positions on the yard, and simple math dictated that one of the four assigned would be white. I volunteered at the library before the sergeant in charge of the yard hired me. I worked there for weeks and got to know the sergeant and the white librarian whose release date was two months later. During those two months, even though the sergeant knew me and knew that I was putting in a lot of volunteer time in the stacks, when the black and Hispanic librarians returned to the streets, they were replaced by inmates of their respective races.

I was designated porter, even though I performed all the librarians' duties and more. My pay rate was eight cents an hour. The librarians earned eleven cents an hour. But a porter I remained because during the sifting process all inmates were screened for job authorization based on our offenses. An arsonist, for instance, would not be assigned to work in an area where there were incendiary liquids; an inmate who used a knife to perpetrate his crime would not be assigned to kitchen detail. During my job placement screening, three of the warden's staff had copies of my commitment file showing my conviction offenses, the duration of my term, and my medical records. "A lawyer who got caught," one of them snarled. "How much did you steal?" I didn't respond and that escalated the tension in the room. Because my conviction was for grand theft, when selecting a job for me, they asked numerous questions. "Did you use computers to commit your crime?" I responded, "No," though this was before I learned that inmates never touch computers, which made the question all the more interesting. Ultimately the committee of three determined I could only be a porter because I could not be trusted in the warehouse, on outside work details, in the kitchen, or in the canteen. And although I did get the white librarian's job when he left and I asked to be changed from porter to librarian, nothing ever came of that request. The single perk was that the library had a porcelain toilet with a seat and a door to close for a rare few moments of privacy.

Gambling Pools

Although not sanctioned by the correctional system, anytime there was a major sports or news event, a gambling pool was set up. The A-B race rule applied to gambling pools to avoid any underhanded and interracial contentions that might develop.

One of the more bizarre gambling pools took place on September 21, 2005. That day the national news coverage was focused on Jet Blue flight 292 as it circled and finally approached Los Angeles International Airport with its front landing gear turned horizontal to the craft's hull. Theories arose in favor of the landing gear holding or collapsing, causing certain disaster. Immediately A-B gambling pools sprang up on the yard: odds were set for the safe landing of the plane versus total disaster befalling the flight's passengers and crew. The proceeds of the pool—bags of chips, toothpaste, spices, packets of tuna, toothbrushes—were rapidly paid to the winners in the A-B pools once the plane landed safely at LAX.

Laundry Machines, Clothing Irons, and Murder

The yard at Ironwood had one washing machine and one dryer. When they were working, 250 men shared the machines, sent their dirty clothes out to the prison laundry, or washed their own clothing in empty lard buckets obtained from the kitchen. A sign-up sheet was available to reserve a day and time to use the machines, and there were no A-B racial restrictions. Men of all colors and ethnicities shared the same washing machine to wash their dirty clothes and the same dryer to dry them.

What seemed right and normal, however, was turned upside and backward when inmates chose to iron their clothing, particularly before a weekend visitation. There were A-B irons for clothing that had been washed in racially integrated laundry machines. This sort of mind-set floated around the prison yard in its own hazy logic.

For example, men who murdered but did not rape their wives or girlfriends were tolerated, but men who murdered a child were not. Prison justice was often enacted to further punish these offenders. However, a man who killed his pregnant wife or girlfriend causing the unborn child to die was accepted as though he had murdered only the woman, not a child. That is why Scott Peterson, serving a life sentence for the murder of his wife and their unborn child and facing the death penalty, was accepted by the other condemned prisoners at San Quentin prison.

Barber Equipment

Combs and electric clippers were designated A or B. Scissors and razor-blades were not used by inmate barbers. Good call. There were many skilled buzz barbers in whatever yard I was assigned. They styled and maintained prison grooming standards, which determined length of hair and the amount of facial hair allowed. The regulations were strict but not often enforced.

I had my hair regularly cut by an inmate named Chano. The prison value for the service was fifty cents or a bag of chips or an ice-cream bar on canteen day. Chano, a Hispanic, could give haircuts only to those in the A racial category, never B. Likewise, a B barber was restricted to cutting only B racial category inmates' hair.

Bathroom and Showers

Racial rituals for bathrooms and showers depended on where one was physically housed in a prison. From my experience, the more crowded and disgusting a housing unit, the more racially restrictive the rituals. In these circumstances, there were specific A and B toilet bowls, sinks, and water fountains. We had no urinals, just the ubiquitous stainless-steel dumpsters with no separately attached seat.

Walking the Track

Walking the track was a social activity. Walking the track, alone, feeling the freedom of relative movement, rejuvenated body and mind. During the shifting and sorting process, going outside to walk or exercise was allowed three times a week. The rest of the time was spent in a nine-by-six-foot two-man cell. The rigidity of the cement walls stood in defiant opposition to human beings' natural curiosity and need for freedom of movement. Walking the track meant being free to walk as fast as you wanted, when you wanted, and anywhere you wanted. A two-man cell had enough room to walk four and a half steps in one direction at a time before hitting a wall, so the track represented incarcerated freedom.

White Monopoly, Black Scrabble, and *Johnson v. California*

John Steinbeck's *Travels with Charley* records stories of the author's 1960 road trip across America with his poodle. As the duo entered the South, Steinbeck noted his feelings of discomfort. The history of the violence of enforced inequality and segregation weighed heavily on his words: "Beyond my failings as a racist, I knew I was not wanted in the South. When people are engaged in something they are not proud of, they do not want witnesses. In fact, they come to believe the witness causes the trouble."[5]

A credible investigation by any objective observer would reveal some startling state-sanctioned racist practices in California's prisons. What did institutionalized racism look like fifty-one years after *Brown v. Board of Education*[6] and eleven years after the demise of apartheid in South Africa? Full exposure was a ticket back in time to the South of Steinbeck's book. I thought race-neutral screening should start at reception by asking short-term inmates if they are agreeable to placement in a segregation-free (seg-free) institution and designating certain prison facilities as fully integrated for housing seg-free inmates. An incentive to ensure successful completion of a seg-free term, such as additional time off a sentence, better sports programs, or more social interaction programs could be offered. Such a policy would not be without precedent: California allows a 15 percent sentence reduction as well as better meals and living conditions for eligible inmates who volunteer for fire-camp duty. Establishing a race-sensitive training program for correctional officers assigned to seg-free prisons and carefully screening officers for racial neutrality would go a long way toward helping as well, creating a superior approach to the century-old segregation scourge in California's prisons. Such a program would allow for the study of how to broaden the seg-free prison cultures and how to accommodate the likely demand for additional seg-free prisons. A step-by-step approach would also permit prison officials to clearly identify those inmates whose negative racial attitudes are entrenched beyond likely change, and who should remain in segregated prisons for safety reasons.

But in my time in prison, all social activity was A-B racially sensitive and strictly enforced. I could not walk the yard with B people without coming under the scrutiny of the white car representatives, the inmates that reported anything of importance to the race's holder of the keys. Ironically, if I was helping a black man with a legal matter, I could sit down with him in the B seating area in the day room with impunity. However, if we walked outside of the physical structure of the prison, we could not talk about the legal matter, and we could not walk the track together.

This situation struck an especially harsh chord with me. It made no sense, and like the other rituals, felt aggravating and just dumb. Racism, in prison, choked the freedom of opportunity to learn about and respect people of other races and reinforced ancient prejudices.

These racial rituals prompted me to find some meaning to the time-wasting, energy-consuming, mind-boggling racism I encountered every day. I pondered the situation and could never find anything good in the state-sanctioned segregation. Inmates, prison administrators, and guards had fallen into racial rituals that the United States Supreme Court had struck down as unconstitutional decades ago. California prisons were a throwback to the pre–separate "but" equal rules rejected in the landmark *Brown v. Board of Education* in 1954.

The double bind of the problem circumscribed all logic. Any objection to any racial ritual would find the dissenter the object of ridicule and scorn from both inmates and staff for "starting something" or "rocking the boat." This reversal of logic was dangerous when the staff played the race card.

I recorded in my journal about the guards' manipulation of the racial tensions on the yard. During my incarceration, there was a strict smoking policy. Smoking was permitted outside; the canteen sold cans of tobacco and rolling paper. The ban on indoor smoking was lightly enforced. The place smelled like cigarette smoke; the air was often foul with secondhand smoke. Complaints to the guards were met with no concern. Inmates use a Form 602 Inmate/Parolee Appeal Form to lodge written complaints, and failure to enforce the indoor smoking ban was a perfect issue. A dozen nonsmoking inmates with like minds filed a 602 appeal and there was a strong fear of retaliation by the smokers even though 602s were supposed to be confidential.

One of the inmates who filed a 602 had a lung condition that was aggravated by secondhand smoke. Fox was a tall, athletically built, soft-spoken black man known for not suppressing his opinions. Fox stored raw anger in every cell of his body. I established a trusted talking relationship with him mostly by listening to what he had pent up inside. He filed a 602 appeal requesting that the nonsmoking rule be enforced. Within a few hours, Fox was confronted by the black car troubleshooters. They wanted him to withdraw the 602 immediately. The confidentiality of Fox's 602 had been breached by an administrative guard who reported Fox's 602 to his Mexican clerk, who, predictably, reported the filing of the 602 to the Mexican car. The Mexican car then confronted the black car key holder demanding that he confront Fox to withdraw the 602 or there would be a racial war. The rationale for this chain of events was that if the already existing nonsmoking policy was actually enforced as the result of a black man's complaint, they, the Mexicans (and it followed, the whites, too) would be unnecessarily "penalized."

These dramas took place all the time and made my head spin. Goodbye to common sense and the law. I'd plunk myself down on my bunk and stare at the ceiling, visiting the familiar accumulation of dust on the duct system and the water stains, one of which was shaped like Donald Duck. And then came a force from outside that was about to lift me out of the race time warp in which I lived.

In 2005, the United States Supreme Court decided a case that directly addressed racial segregation in California's prisons. In a five-to-three opinion, it cast a verbal bolt of lightning to the heart of the racial segregation rules and rituals I have described. That case was *Johnson v. California.*[7]

California inmate Garrison S. Johnson was a black man who voiced objection to racial segregation rituals. His attorney, Bert H. Deixler, a tenacious and competent lawyer, handled the reins of the case that went all the way to the United States Supreme Court. Johnson's case raised the question of whether the California Department of Corrections, unlike every other state, could continue its practice of routine blanket racial segregation of its prisoners in making temporary cellmate assignments. The issue was framed narrowly and did not address most of the racial ritual rules I've described, but the language of the decision was instructive and binding.

Johnson argued that the state used *race* as the primary criteria for housing assignments. His legal argument was that California's admitted racial segregation cell assignment policy violated his Fourteenth Amendment right to equal protection of the law. The attorneys for the state of California argued that the practice of segregating in this fashion was constitutionally protected because it protected inmates against violence.

A huge number of men and women were affected in the way Johnson was. In oral arguments on November 2, 2004, Bert Deixler told the justices that "the unitary practice in question here was applied more than 350,000 times last year, not just to the 40,000 new prisoners entering the California system, but to all 72,000 returning parolees and hundreds of thousands of transfer prisoners such as the petitioner in this case, Garrison Johnson, a petitioner who had been housed for more than 15 years in the California prison system."[8]

Mr. Deixler illustrated the uniqueness of California's de facto segregation policy when he told the court, "Other States use a random assignment circumstance, and giving no consideration whatever to race."

Justice Ginsburg posed an elucidating question: "Were there any incidents in California's prisons of same cellmates of different races having episodes of violence? Or was this an old policy? Were there incidents that led to the development of the policy?"

Mr. Deixler replied "Justice Ginsburg, one of the interesting things about the record in this case is that the State of California has been unable to identify a single incident of a . . . of interracial violence between cellmates. The record is bereft of that kind of information."

Justice Scalia left his disdain about the racial issue on the record: "What is . . . what is sacrosanct about the . . . about the constitutional right not to be subjected to racial stereotype? There are a lot of other constitutional rights that people in prison give up. That's one of the consequences of committing a crime and being sent to prison, the most fundamental constitutional right, the right to . . . to walk around and . . . and not be seized. Why . . . why is it that this . . . this one constitutional right cannot yield to what prison authorities believe is . . . is a useful, not necessarily essential, but a useful means of . . . of maintaining order in prison?"[9]

Justice Scalia's position was not supported by the record as Mr. Deixler had informed Justice Ginsburg.

The *Johnson* case scratched the surface of the chilling effects on prisoners' rights as a result of decades of racial segregation. The decision did not touch on the permanence of the housing policy. It is my hope that the ultimate holding in the case will provide guidance concerning the degrading pernicious racial rituals I've written about here.

The *Johnson* case illustrates the placement of judicial limitations on broader issues in response to a limited set of facts that shed light on a systemic problem. I read as much as I could find on the issues surrounding the case and came to the conclusion that the case did give a glimpse into the racial segregation I experienced.

The issue of racial segregation was put to rest in 1968 when the Supreme Court ruled in *Lee v. Washington* that Alabama's statutes requiring racial separation in its prisons violated the Fourteen Amendment. However, the legal hair being split in the *Johnson* case was that California does not mandate segregation in prison. In fact, the California Code of Regulations, Title 15, Section 3004(c) states: "Inmates, parolees, and employees will not subject other persons to any form of discrimination because of race."

On February 23, 2005, the Supreme Court, in a five-to-three decision authored by Justice Sandra Day O'Connor, declined to rule directly on the constitutionality of the reception practice of segregation. The case was remanded (sent back to) the Ninth Circuit Court of Appeals to invoke a strict legal scrutiny test to determine Fourteenth Amendment due process applicability. In writing for the majority, Justice O'Connor stated, "We rejected the notion that separate can be equal . . . fifty years ago in *Brown v. Board of Education*, and we refuse to resurrect it today." The majority left the issue of segregating gang members or violent individuals from other inmates up to prison authorities. The state's own studies, presented at the court of appeals level, supported the notion that violence in the prisons was proportional to the prevalence of gangs and not from racial tension.

Justice John Paul Stevens, in his dissent, stated that he would have struck down California's policy, "given the inherent indignity of segregation and its shameful historical connotations." Justices Clarence Thomas and Antonin Scalia, in separate dissents, stated that the entire matter should be left up to prison officials. Scalia rationalized that the segregation was "temporary and [inmates] are kept separate for the time which the California prison believes it needs in order to assure that there won't be violence, and then once that assurance is given, the races are mixed."[10]

Scalia and Thomas were heavily swayed by the argument in the brief filed by state Attorney General Bill Lockyer: "All other aspects of an inmate's life (after allegedly determining propensity for racial violence) in prison both while at the reception center and afterwards are managed without reference to his race or that of his fellow inmates. There is no distinction based on race for jobs, meals, yard and recreation time, or vocational and educational assignments."[11]

When I read that, I had to wonder where the attorney general got his erroneous assumptions that he caramelized into "facts."

Johnson v. California was heard in oral argument before the Supreme Court in November 2004. A month later, a California correctional officer filed a whistle-blower's complaint stating that state officials lied to the Supreme Court about segregation in the state's prison system. The whistle-blower contended that the attorney general and Department of

Corrections officials also lied about the extent that racial classification was used in setting prison policies. The complaint sought an official investigation of the situation by the state auditor.

Here was a world of racial rituals given license by official inaction. In a prison system that otherwise monitored and restricted an inmate's conduct, movement, and pattern of behavior through interventions ranging from disciplinary write-ups to use of deadly force, the California Department of Corrections allowed the fires of racism to rage in its prisons with impunity. The ratified social behaviors are not recorded in any official document but are knitted into the passively accepted moral code inmates live by in the mainline. The racial code of conduct is enforced by a system of "justice" devised by the prisoners, the existence of which is common knowledge to prison administrators.

Ironically, under the state-sanctioned racial code, if Scalia and Thomas were serving time in the same California prison, they would not be permitted to share a cell or bunk with each other. They would be restricted as to where they could eat in the dining room; Thomas would be relegated to the B section, Scalia to the A. Inmates Scalia and Thomas would have television privileges, but in distinctly separate areas. A game of chess between the two dissenters would violate the strict racial code. All board games are restricted to intraracial competition. Games are actually labeled by race: "White Monopoly" or "Black Scrabble." If inmates Thomas and Scalia agreed to walk the prison yard together, such an association would constitute a breach of the rigid racial divide and likely result in physical retribution, otherwise known as *taxing*, meted out by their fellow inmates. Similarly, Scalia would be allowed to give Thomas sealed food items such as chips or candy bars (never food from his dining hall tray), but the former could never openly accept any food from Thomas.

Fifty-two years after *Brown*, separate and unequal is still the rule oppressing the economically disadvantaged and people of color. Changes in racial perspectives happen slowly, but it's my belief that the time to start the change in California prisons is well past due.

CHAPTER SEVEN

Respect

The minute you said that thing about the Rican girls . . . if I was you I'd ask transfer for protection . . . cause if you stay on this floor you're asking to die . . . you'll be committing involuntary suicide.

— Miguel Piñero, *Short Eyes*

RESPECT IS A COMPLEX phenomenon in prison, and to survive, it must be understood. Respect goes hand-in-hand with humiliation and shame but is broader in scope and primarily refers to interactions between inmates. Respect includes all the common societal dictates from the outside; that is, society teaches us that respect means consideration for others and treating people courteously and with kindness. Respect applies in family, social, and business situations. As children, most of us are taught to respect our parents and other authoritarian figures—teachers, religious leaders, political leaders. We are taught to respect our belongings, our bodies, and those abstract concepts we call rules and laws. But this understanding of respect is too simplistic for surviving prison. In prison, if you disrespect another inmate's sock, and thereby its owner, by accidently walking on it, you're in trouble. "Hey, dumb fuck—you just gonna bounce by after disrespecting my sock?" Sometimes no words will quell fired-up language. Sometimes misplaced but vicious anger is unleashed—over a sock.

In prison respect is sometimes counterintuitively framed as disrespect that you don't see coming. I quickly learned that there are unwritten rules about disrespecting a fellow inmate, his race or culture, his belongings, his work ethic, his neighborhood/territory/street (pathway past a bunk or locker); the list is endless. It is possible to disrespect music, walk or gait, intelligence, another's "old lady," you name it. Early on I learned to measure my words when I talked to inmates about anything personal they came to me to discuss. If a guy's wife had divorce papers filed and served on him, regardless what he called the woman who was divorcing him, when we discussed the matter, I never used disparaging language about his "old lady."

Personal radio use exemplifies how respect turns to disrespect in a flash. A wood asks a Mexican to turn down the volume on his Latin music station. The request, rather simple on its face, can turn to this instantly: "So you don't like my music—you insult my culture," at which point the wood either engages and escalates the conversation or dismisses it as a no-win conversation where there are no words to get out. This happened to me when I asked a patron of the library to turn off his radio. He turned it louder. When I ignored him, he left the library.

Sometimes inmates were just plain mean and tossed aside rules of respect in order to gain advantage, especially when it came to food. I learned that one difficult morning as I described in my journal:

> We were denied breakfast this morning by inmate porters because our bright light (in the cell) was not on. I was up all morning and there was no usual announcement to "get ready for chow and turn on cell light if you want breakfast." The inmate porters took advantage of the mistake and hoarded as many breakfast trays as they could for themselves and their buddies. I can see them in a corner of the dayroom devouring my breakfast like filthy vermin, caring less about anyone else being hungry.

—Journal entry, January 11, 2004

The influence and power of gangs on their members was immediately evident. I watched and studied gang members' behaviors to try to understand the powerful cohesiveness of gangster mentality. I experienced that mentality immediately upon my arrival into the prison system. Gangs, I quickly saw, were respect-by-force groups. Members advanced in their gang by doing work on behalf of the whole. The most valuable work had criminal components that exposed members to long prison terms if caught. The work done for a gang was reflected in the tattoo earned by a member who had *earned his stripes* by doing work.

The gang mentality parallels the *cat's paw* theory of discrimination within employment law. The theory borrows from a seventeenth-century fable in which a conniving monkey convinces an unwitting cat to reach into a fire to grab some roasting chestnuts. Duped, the cat burns its paw, and the monkey enjoys the chestnuts and leaves none for the cat. The work done by gang members—exposing themselves to danger and confinement while offering anonymity to those in charge—is a common theme. Those inside reminded me of the faceless destruction caused by drones in today's fields of battle.

Arriving on a new yard was always terrifying. You always arrived during the day to ensure an extra level of safety for prison staff. We were always unloaded from the buses in complete silence, and the moment both feet hit the ground, the handcuffs linked to our leg chains were removed and orders were given to line up in single file and continue to "shut the fuck up." Renewed freedom to use our arms and legs quelled the verbal abuse, and we entered the prison yard through a sally port. The sensation was like being led into a lion's den. You can't get tired of the politics every day brings. The rules of respect often change when the politics on the yard shift after newly arriving inmates replace paroled inmates. The personality mixes are constantly churning, creating a vapor that can be ignited by the most innocuous spark.

Upon arriving on a new yard or returning to a yard, security reprocessing began. It reminded me of the TSA clearing passengers into an airport terminal—a "sterile zone" exists—once a passenger leaves that zone, if he returns he'll be scanned and searched again. Prison was like that. When a bus filled with inmates arrived on the yard, herds of existing inmates moved toward the bus and lined up against the chain-link fence to view and harass the newcomers. New arrivals were always of interest, and stares and comments were unyielding. Men were scanning for their fellow gang members, for hated foes, for old acquaintances from past rodeos, for the weak and meek they might exploit. The sizing-up was instantaneous, with none of TSA's technology—inmates scan with gut reactions and stored memories.

This, I learned fast, is *ghost time*, the best time not to be seen. Here are the rules: Don't make eye contact. Look straight ahead. Ignore the comments, jives, and insults.

Once someone yelled out, "Hey Woody Allen," and didn't stop. "Hey, look, that guy looks like fuckn' Woody Allen. Look, dig that shit—Hey

Woody, hey baby, what you packing for me? I come visit you Woody!"
I quickly straightened my posture, slowly removed my round-shaped
glasses and made only peripheral eye contact. The reference to packing meant contraband I might be carrying up my butt to share and
earn safety—those items were usually tobacco, drugs, syringes, coffee, and other items that can fit in a waterproof baggy for storing in
a tight space. I didn't drink coffee and did not smoke or deal with
drugs. I always had an empty cavity, which frequently displeased the
shot callers for the white race. "What the fuck good are you anyway,
Roseman?" I had to fill in that blank really fast.

Once a shot caller saw me as unworthy, I had to find ways to earn
respect. I used my ability to read, write, and listen, and my legal skills
honed in years of practice. I quickly learned to determine what I could do
for the shot caller and his closest lieutenants. Reading and responding
to letters was on the top of the list, followed by calculating their sentences, and if they were not correct, preparing a Request for Interview
petition to the administration for a sentencing review. Once my first sentence calculation was approved for another inmate, my street cred rose
through the ceiling. My respect stock soared. I had earned my stripes.

Groupthink and Anti-Semitism

Everyone has had groupthink experiences.[1] If you've worked on a committee or planning team striving to find a consensus within the group,
you understand groupthink. Election returns are a measure of groupthink about a candidate or proposition. Kids learn to socialize using
groupthink, in good and bad ways. What brand backpack a student has
can elicit acceptance or rejection, depending on the groupthink at that
school about what constitutes a cool backpack.

Housing in cramped quarters quickly arouses small talk. And I knew,
from practicing law, not to ignore that small talk. Knowing what was
said, when, and by whom are vital elements that most trial lawyers
recognize and cement into their brains. So when I was assigned to cell
A-II at Ironwood where there were four cots, one vacant with my name
on it, my acceptance assimilation radar went up. This was where being
a ghost was tricky business. An inmate never knows how much he can
show. Predators await weak inmates, ready to hone in and exploit. Gay
men relegate themselves to doing "women's work"—another's laundry

and ironing, for instance—since the consensus is that gay men are safe when performing female chores.

I saw this in action at the Orange County Jail in October 2003. Cell A-11 housed three Hispanic men from different Santa Ana neighborhoods. Two were young gang members, not hard-core gangsters; they had joined their neighborhood gang to earn protection for their families from other gangs. One was a drug runner who got caught but would not rat on the others involved. He was twenty-one and lost, like so many kids I met inside.

The second guy was twenty and had stabbed his stepfather in the neck while the stepfather was in an alcoholic rage. The inmate's mother told police the attack was unprovoked. The inmate said she lied to protect her children, since the stepfather housed and fed the family. This broken kid had fifteen years before parole eligibility.

The third guy was twenty-seven and referred to himself as *state raised*. He had had too many devastating twists and turns in his life for me to remember, but I do remember he started being state raised in juvenile hall. His mother was sixteen years old when he was born, and she wound up homeless. To stay warm at night during the cold Orange County winters, she would take him to one particular big-box store where the night closing security procedures had a "blind spot," enabling them to sleep inside the store. Before they left in the morning, his mother had him put on layers of new underwear, socks, jackets and trousers. They would walk out of the store wearing their new wardrobes. One morning when he was thirteen years old, they were caught, and what followed was an unsettling life in myriad foster homes, which set the stage for a life in prison. He had just returned to prison after thirteen arrests for shoplifting and two new burglary convictions. Being state raised in California sucked the potential out of children, usually until they were plopped into the correctional system, at which point they had no idea what the world might offer beyond their limited scope.

As each of my new cellmates sat on their bunks and took turns telling me their stories, they were sizing me up to see if I was a fit. I usually offered little. I asked a lot of questions. In my first days in prison, I'd ask about the phone policy, showers, times for chow—basic stuff. In my more learned stage, after I'd been inside for six months, my questions reflected the level of sophistication to which I'd risen: Who's the

shot caller? What's the race policy for bathrooms? Are there any books
or pieces of books for sharing? Who should I watch out for and why?

In these groupthink situations I always won the cellmates' consensus
that I was no danger. If I felt challenged in a way I didn't understand,
I faded into ghost status. Sometimes, however, I was caught off guard.

I'd grown up aware of anti-Semitism but never experienced its
harshness in any personal way. I'd cringe when I heard someone in the
midst of negotiating a price saying, "Don't Jew me down." But beyond
that, I had little direct experience with anti-Semitism.

> There's a 60-year old guy—Pops—whose bunk is right by me. If I'm
> on my back and looking down to my left, I have a clear shot of him.
> His arms and legs are long and lanky and move at right angles like an
> insect. He's from Mississippi and proud to be from the same town as
> David Duke, and the fact that he was born on 4/20—Hitler's birth-
> day. He says the word "Jew" in a way that makes the word sound
> dirty, disgusting, and vile. I don't like him.

—Letter to my sister, December 9, 2003

I'd never seen or heard such a specimen of human life until I met Pops
in December 2003 at Wasco, my reception prison after Orange County
Jail. I didn't really "meet" him; it took him a few days even to acknowledge my existence. I was in a pod of eight men in four closely situated
bunk beds. The space between our bunks was our street. One afternoon
I caught Pops looking up at me from his bunk with one eye covered—
it was rolling and bulging like a grasshopper. When he looked at me
with both eyes, I saw they were small glittering eyes that gleamed with
malice. I was to see a lot of that look during the early part of my term,
in the days before I had earned my respect on the yard. Pops's voice did
not fit his tall frame—it was high-pitched like Mickey Mouse's when
you were expecting the gravelly voice of Long John Silver.

> He looks like a human grasshopper. His head ratchets like an insect's.
> Long spiny fingers, skinny legs, and a big, big gut. He cackles a lot
> about nothing special as long as it's something negative. My lower
> Bunkie, Angel, told me that Pops had done 30 years in Angola and
> had another 20 years of California time to do stemming from the
> same murder. I was puzzled by Angola—he'd done time in Africa? It

didn't make sense. I didn't yet know Angola was a maximum penitentiary in Louisiana.

—Journal entry, December 2003

Pops finally broke his silence toward me right before chow on December 9, 2003. He was talking about Angola and what a harsh prison system it was. The conditions were horrible, and only the worst of the worst were confined there. "You been to Angola?" he shot at me from his lower bunk. He didn't use my name, but it was clear he meant me. The remaining seven of us on our street froze for a second. I gave a stupid answer, under the circumstances: "Nope, never been to Africa." There was a hush and then a howl from everyone who had heard me. Mickey's crackling voice bore through with a hate-filled darkness as he chortled, "Now don't go Jew on me or I'll gas ya."

What could I say to that? What intelligent repartee could I expect? There were no words to penetrate this level of learned and institutionalized hatred. I chose to disengage myself from the conversation and to fade out of sight and become a ghost.

Respect is both a sword and a shield, depending on how it's packaged. On the streets, the rules of respect, in many instances, mirror those on the inside. The opposite of road rage is, for example, respecting the rules of the road. In conjunction with state and federal penal systems, laws, ordinances, and the like are intended to keep communities peaceful. Only persons found guilty of crimes are punished for their actions. However, on the inside, the errant conduct of one is cause to punish all—which further fractures harmony between the races and weakens the power of the contained to garner a concerted effort for common goals. When you hear about prison riots over living conditions, you can count on the fact that all races were thoroughly engaged in a common goal—something very rare in the prison environment.

Because of the way humans are wired, confined people will use respect as a vague cultural standard. This counterintuitive way of thinking was a big piece of surviving. You get to know your place, and if it's comfortable to be in that space, prison time will pass as fast as it can. Groupthink is a total crapshoot. One personality can poison an entire yard. On the other hand, the right mix of men reduces stress and incidents of violence. You just don't know what the day will bring.

I don't know what became of Pops. After his barrage of anti-Semitism, I tried to come to some understanding of what, if anything, the incident taught me. I learned a very important lesson at this early stage of my incarceration: you have to choose very carefully whom to befriend. Some men I met along the way need to be incarcerated, and thus society is made a safer place, literally. I met a man with eleven years down who killed someone during an armed robbery. The guy reasoned that his victim's pleas for mercy made the victim weak, thereby justifying taking him out. I spoke to this guy at Wasco an hour before chow. The conversation was so upsetting, I gave my entire tray to a goat.

CHAPTER EIGHT

Contact and Communication

Receiving mail is one of the highlights of an inmate's day especially when it's from a good friend such as you. Continue to consider me a captive audience for your letter writing cravings . . . it's better than chocolate.

—Letter to a former client and friend, December 18, 2003

I N PRISON, THERE ARE many forms of contact and communication. Physical contact—the human desire to be touched—exists in the form of horseplay, massages, and haircuts. Inmates give other inmates haircuts with tools provided by the administration, and I looked forward to mine because the tactile component was pleasantly stimulating. Upon the slightest touch of my hair, chills ran down my neck and back. I've noticed this same sensation when I get my hair cut now, but it is not as profound as it was when I was starved for simple human touch.

Visitations are the real highlight of contact and communication in prison. The style of visitation depends upon the inmate's disciplinary record and level of security in which he is housed. Visitations are either contact or noncontact. The CDCR's official policy is to encourage visitation with inmates, as their publications state:

Visiting a family member or friend who is in prison is an important way to maintain connections during incarceration and enhances the prisoner's success both while in prison and after release. The California

Department of Corrections and Rehabilitation (CDCR) recognizes the importance of visitation and encourages families and friends to visit as often as their circumstances allow.

—*CDCR: Visiting a Friend or Loved One in Prison (2015)*

Contact visits take place in a secured, locked room such as a multipurpose room within the prison compound. During contact visits, inmates sit at tables and are under constant scrutiny by guards. A brief hug and kiss are permitted at the start and end of the visit. Inmates' hands must always be visible above the table, and any prolonged physical contact is forbidden. Still, the sheer excitement of a visit minimized the impact of these rules for me.

Noncontact visitations take place one-on-one with a Plexiglas window separating the inmate from his visitor and communication taking place through old-fashioned telephone receivers. The amount of time allowed for any visit is determined by an inmate's privilege class. Privilege class was determined by the crime committed, the amount of time remaining on a sentence, the history of violence, and the history of importation of contraband into the prison system. Of course, during these visits phone lines were tapped and prison personnel were free to listen in on the conversations. In this way, the administration learned about potential problems involving rats, kites, and the movement of contraband from the streets to the prison.

Married inmates with good behavior records are permitted conjugal/ family visits. These visits take place on weekends in separate, secured housing facilities, away from the general prison population. I saw how important these visits were to keeping families intact and hopeful about the future. For these visits, inmates preordered and paid for food supplies from a menu. When other inmates knew someone was going to have a weekend visit, the customary conversation was all about getting laid. I was granted family visits with my parents and as a result always had to correct the well-wishers, letting them know it was my parents who were coming to visit. That shut them up.

In an e-mail dated December 12, 2004, my father, who was eightyone at the time, wrote to friends and family, accurately reporting his and my mother's experience, and mine, during a family visit:

Hi All.

We are back from our Mark visit. It went very well considering where our family visit took place. Mark looks great and feels great. This family visit was like a vacation to him. They put us up in a single home unit with a large yard in the back that was surrounded by cyclone fencing and wire. We were locked in with a large lock and they have the key. . . . The amenities were to be desired as we had no utensils to eat with, but finally got them. There was a sink, frig, microwave, but no cups either, but came the next day. . . . Our food was ordered in advance from their so-called menu list, you should not know from that, and paid for in advance. There was no charge for the living quarters. The meals were brought in all at once the first day, such as frozen meals, milk, soda, water, and orange and apple juice. We also had oranges, apples, yogurt, burritos, small pizza pies, bagels and cream cheese and popcorn.

We did get linens and towels that were very rough. Made our own beds and our own cleaning. We even had a television. Brought two word games which we played. His lady Sgt. in charge of E yard brought us a menorah for Chanukah and so lit the candles. Mark was surprised that they gave him matches to light them as matches are not allowed.

We had a phone in the room that could only be answered by Mark. In fact, they called several times a day to check on him via phone and then had him go to the gate so he could be physically seen. Same routine happened at night at 11PM, 2AM, 5AM, 7 AM, for which he had to present himself to be physically seen.

Any adult wishing to visit a prisoner must first obtain approval from CDCR by completing a Visitor Questionnaire (CDCR Form 106) and making an application. Besides my parents, I sent these forms to my sons, my sister and brother-in-law, and friends. A completed Form 106 authorizes the CDCR to conduct a background check of potential visitors; they check for arrests and convictions when processing the application and will deny approval to visit if the check indicates an arrest or conviction not listed by the applicant on the questionnaire.

Every California prison has visiting on Saturdays, Sundays, and four holidays during each calendar year: New Year's Day, the Fourth of July, Thanksgiving Day, and Christmas Day. Upon arrival at Ironwood for visitation, visitors are patted down and their belongings are searched. Visitors must remove all outer clothing (jackets, sweaters, vests), shoes, and any jewelry that will set off the metal detector. This search is to detect contraband of any kind—weapons, drugs, drug paraphernalia, or anything that can be turned into a deadly weapon.

One visit with my childhood friend and her husband illustrates the seriousness of the search. Gail and Steve arrived on time for screening and processing for a morning visit. Gail did not pass the metal detector test three times. She was asked if she wanted to forfeit the visit, which she declined. A female guard took her to a private room for a strip search, down to her underwear. The upper part of her body squawked as the portable metal detector insisted she was toting metal. The culprit turned out to be the WMD underwires of Gail's new bra, and the only way she was allowed to visit me was if the underwires were removed from her bra. She agreed, and we had a good visit. To this day we still laugh about this. I still owe her a new bra.

Those inmates who earn the privilege are permitted to make collect phone calls out, but inmates are never allowed to receive calls except in the rarest of emergencies. Each evening we would sign up for phone privileges for a particular time slot. We lined up in racially dictated lines to sign up for the next day's phone privileges; each collect call was limited to fifteen minutes. Phone calls are monitored—as all inmates and those they speak to are told in recorded messages that accompany a phone call from any institution. I was surprised to discover that the phones were not designated for use by color—that is, any race could use any telephone. Phone conversations can be hazed in code to pass on news about a rat or to communicate information from one location of the prison system to another. My family and friends followed an unwritten rule: no complaining, no drama, no crying. Rather, we enjoyed these moments of voice contact. Inside, that intangible contact transformed an inmate to a man, someone who had people outside who loved and cared for him and his well-being.

Unfortunately, the exorbitant cost of collect calls charged by contractors to the CDCR made such contacts almost impossible. My parents and friends paid rates between fifteen and seventeen dollars per minute, which came to as much as two hundred fifty-five dollars per call. We usually talked for ten minutes. The excessive cost proved an impediment to keeping families together, and so despite the CDCR policy, the hurdles to connection were many.

After pressure from families and prisoner's-rights groups, in February 2014, the Federal Communications Commission passed new laws imposing a limit of twenty-five cents per minute for debit calling and twenty-one cents per minute for collect calls. At those levels, the cost of a fifteen-minute call was reduced by as much as 80 percent, to between three and four dollars. Now many families will no longer have to choose between talking to their loved ones in prison and paying their utility bills, and society will benefit from the decreased rates of recidivism that family contact brings. FCC Chairman Tom Wheeler and Commissioners Jessica Rosenworcel and Mignon Clyburn are quoted as saying: "These families can now afford to keep in touch because the era of unreasonable and unjust phones rates has ended."[1]

Tattoos

I spent 45 minutes at the library looking for a picture of a howling wolf. A guy wanted to use the picture as a guide for a tattoo artist—he wanted the picture on his chest.

—*Letter to my parents, April 18, 2004*

Many talented people are locked up in prisons, and among them are the tattoo artists, who are always in demand. Inside there seemed to be a universal impulse to embellish the human body, and as a communicative art form, the prison tattoo served different purposes. Tattoos are hieroglyphics that the learned eye can read and decipher to understand the intended message. I studied, and I learned.

One day, as I was lying on my back on my lower bunk, I heard a fast tap on the iron railing of the double-decker bunk. I recognized the face. He looked pale and frightened. "I'd like to, ahhh . . . enter your street . . . talk," he stammered. I waved him in and told him he could sit at the far end of my bunk.

His name was Alex. He was a skinhead with something on his mind. His facial expressions and body movements indicated conflict. He had come with a letter as a pretense—"It's something legal," he said—but when I looked I saw it was a form letter for a prepaid legal service. I wanted to ask him the meaning of number fourteen, but instead he told me that one of his comrades had a picture of his wife next to his bed. "So?" I asked. "Well," Alex said, "she looks Mexican." He went on to tell me that the commander of the skinheads on the yard wanted this guy messed up and the picture destroyed. Alex had been designated as one of the point men assigned to watch for guards in the area before the planned early morning attack. Alex didn't have the cold and callous racist gene in his DNA that his comrades carried. I shook my head. I could only agree that he was caught in a Catch-22, and I wished him luck. Early the next morning a skinhead was dragged out of his top bunk and targeted as the victim of a boot party. He was stomped and kicked with prison-fashioned steel-toed boots, and afterwards rolled out to Ad Seg (Administrative Segregation, also known as protective custody) for his own protection.

Alex did tell me about *fourteen*. It represents fourteen words from a quote by a Nazi leader who died in prison doing a 190-year sentence for killing a Jewish talk show host: "We must secure the existence of our people and a future for White Children."

Every car had its own rules for identifying territory. When approved through some unclear qualification of doing "work" for the gang, the place from which an inmate hails is tattooed on his stomach. This is called a *rocker*. That tattoo signals that the wearer had the right to *rock your area*, or turf.

But there was a hitch. At least one existing gang member had to cosign for the new guy, which put the gang member's butt on the line if the new guy didn't perform to standards. For example, if the gang was engaged in a fight or an all-out riot, the new member was expected to jump into the battle. If he didn't, the new member and the cosigner—who was likely engaged in battle—would be *smashed* by the gang members who had been in the fight. And there were degrees of being smashed, a rule enforced by every race. Thankfully the white car relieved me of this obligation because of my age and the obvious fact that I wasn't made for fighting on behalf of the whites. Reverse ageism had its benefits. I think, too, that most of my fellow inmates trusted me to keep my mouth shut. I had learned early on to see nothing.

No one is supposed to get letters or any gang tattoos on his first term, though the name of your nineteen-year-old old lady was deemed okay. Likewise, I noticed many inmates with tears tattooed beside their eyes. Some had chains of tears, and I learned that tears meant different things in different parts of the country. In California, a tear represented five years served, while in other areas a single tear meant the wearer had been convicted of murder.

A shot of reality is necessary here. By law, tattoos and tattoo paraphernalia were prohibited by Title 15, California Code of Regulations.

> Inmates shall not tattoo themselves or others, and shall not permit tattoos to be placed on themselves. Inmates shall not remove or permit removal of tattoos from themselves or others.

> —*California Code of Regulations, Title 15, Sec 3315(a)(3)(D), Serious Rule Violations(D) Tattooing or possession of tattoo paraphernalia*

The reasons for the prohibition are many and varied. The primary reason cited by the CDCR is the health concern of spreading hepatitis B and other transferable diseases. Also, tattoos are open books, and their content can be grounds for disharmony among the general population on the yard. Inmates arriving on a yard have their tattoos photographed and digitally inventoried. The photographs are kept in databases to monitor the growth of artwork on an inmate's body during his tenure inside. Theoretically, prison authorities would not have a difficult time proving that tattooing happens all the time, but I never saw the enforcement of the tattoo prohibition. My view is that tattoos are a communication tool used by inmates and gangs and thereby threaten the control of prison management, but enforcement would prove dangerous.

While I was inside, I asked a lot of questions about tattooing and learned a great deal. First, I learned that a tattoo gun must be constructed, and my fellow inmates were tremendously resourceful when it came to fulfilling needs. A motor from a cassette player or hair trimmer was usually used. The motor was fastened to a paper clip or a mechanical pencil. The pencil tube worked as the barrel in which the needle was guided. Making the needle was a critical skill. The point of a guitar string or a straightened spring was sharpened with sandpaper. The tattoo gun was powered by a battery pack or sometimes hooked directly to the inside of a table radio. A volume control knob was often used to control the speed of the needle.

Making the ink was another underground industry upon which prison tattoo artists relied. I watched the process as the tattoo artist set a small pie tin on the floor or in a locker, then placed black plastic chess pieces in the pan and lit them like candles. The next step called for placing a brown paper bag over the smoldering pieces. Soot collected inside the paper bag, and, using a playing card or an ID card, the ink maker scraped out the soot, added water or baby oil, and voilà, you had black ink that remained permanently when used with a tattoo gun. But because the result was always black ink, prison tattoos are not too difficult to spot. They are always black, and the margins are not as defined as those drawn by professional artists using professional tools and inks.

Swastikas, also referred to as *Swazis,* were also prevalent on the yard, and it took me some time to become nonreactive. A large Swazi might cover a man's entire abdomen, from the base of the sternum to below the navel. I never really got used to the sight.

Kites

Another form of communication inside is the kite, a written communiqué that orders punishment against an inmate for some prior action. Kites circulated throughout the prison environment, sometimes sneaked in by a new inmate on the yard who had figured out how to hide the kite during the screening at the sally port. For obvious reasons, kites were secret.

> Last week we had a frightening event. An inmate was badly beaten. He was jumped and bloodied up—not stabbed. This came moments after he and I were talking and I went out onto the yard. He was taken to the hospital and is now in protective custody on another yard. A "kite" (contract) was out for him to settle an old score.
>
> —*Letter to my son Dan, March 26, 2004*

Kites were also evidence of the moment when building gang tensions required an increase in the institution's state of alert. A kite might be, for instance, from an inmate to an administrator, tipping off the administration to the inevitability of a riot in the yard:

> On August 5, 2009, CIM's [California Institution for Men] appeals office received a handwritten note, referred to in inmate slang as a "kite." The kite indicated that one group of inmates would attack another group on the yard at RC East in retaliation for an earlier incident involving the same groups. After corroborating evidence was discovered the next day during routine searches by officers, members of CIM's Investigative Services Unit (ISU) deemed the kite to be credible.[2]

Sign Language

Among the more interesting communication behaviors I witnessed inside was the use of gang sign language. While it's generally known that gangs have their own colors, gangs also have their own signs and sign languages. At one point during my sentence I was being housed temporarily at the CIM. I was in one of its twelve housing units on Facility D where the population far exceeded the maximum two hundred for which it was designed. The units were long, with double bunks along the entire inside perimeter. A floor-to-ceiling wall separated one side of the unit from the other. Inmates could not communicate with inmates on the other side of the wall.

During count time, the usual roar of prison subsided since we were required to sit or lie on our bunks and remain silent. At this time, inmates would sign with members of their gang in their respective languages. They flashed messages with hand, finger, and arm movements that reminded me of a sudden flash of a flock of birds in flight. Hands and arms fluttered in one section, picked up and fluttered to another, and eventually traveled around the wall to the other side. The message on one particular day was to move a homemade barbell that was visible under someone's bunk before it was confiscated. Weightlifting apparatus was considered contraband. And the message was delivered, promptly, efficiently, elegantly. I realized, then, that people will figure out ways to communicate. Everyone inside did.

CHAPTER NINE

How Law School Prepared Me for Prison

Pete playing loud music in the library—just to aggravate me. When I asked him to turn it down, he turned it up. A real jerk, but I don't get support from my coworkers. Ran the situation through IRAC and concluded to shine it on.

—Journal entry, May 24, 2004

I VIVIDLY REMEMBER MY law school orientation. It was August 1975 on the campus of Western State University, Fullerton, California (WSU). The Southern California day was scorching hot. The air conditioning in the school gave perfect relief from the heat but not the anxiety I felt about entering law school. The dean of the school— Maxwell Boas—a bald man who spoke in a nasal tone, welcomed the entering class of some 150 nervous students. I remember feeling the excitement of and the fear about studying law. With my bachelor of science in agriculture from Ohio State University, I knew nothing about what it took to become a lawyer. In 1976, in a classroom full of other students, a creative writing professor at Ohio State University had asked me why I was in the college of agriculture. I always got good grades in that class, but she said, "You should be in law school,

Mr. Roseman," and that planted a seed in my mind, one that came to fruition with my admission to WSU.

That first day the dean made two points about the law school experience that grabbed my attention: (1) the school had a large attrition rate; and, (2) if we made it through, we would know what it meant to "think like a lawyer." I wondered what that meant.

The dean's first point quickly proved true. By the end of the second semester, more than half the students would either voluntarily leave the program or would flunk out. By the end of the second semester, the number of survivors in my class had dropped to just sixty-two. Some simply didn't like the brain squeeze required. We could never lag behind in reading assignments of case law and legal articles, which required intense focus. Law school was like putting together a large jigsaw puzzle in your brain; if you missed a rule of law in a case or particular theory of law—an essential piece of the puzzle—you'd never see the whole picture. With tax and probate law, for instance, I zoned out for lack of interest, and to this day I'm weak in those areas of law. This lack would wind up foreshadowing my aversion to tax matters at Blum & Roseman, leading to my reliance on Melanie for taxes and bookkeeping oversight—which would turn out to be a huge mistake.

But law school also meant sacrifice—greatly limiting social events to study and keep a tunnel vision on school and the constant and pressing reading assignments. In my three years of study at WSU, I read thousands of cases, and I missed birthday parties, anniversaries, reunions, and New Year's Eve celebrations because of the demands I took upon myself to keep up. There is a *click* in the brain that kicks a law student into high gear, and students who didn't experience the click either quit or failed. Luckily for me it clicked.

Reading and analyzing cases and hornbooks (interpretations of the law) gave me the legal fabric for what's called *black-letter law*, the term used to describe the well-established technical legal rules that are no longer subject to reasonable dispute. Some examples are black-letter law of contracts and the black-letter law of criminal law. The common thread of black-letter law eventually merges into a law student's database and becomes a comfortable way of thinking. Without that cohesive fabric, legal studies would be disjointed, burdensome, and mundane. For me, by the end of the second semester, I experienced the flashbulb moment of thinking like a lawyer. I realized that in both civil and criminal law there are logical elements. For example, the basic elements of a contract (civil law) include an offer, an acceptance, and consideration (money, or the relinquishment of a known right). Likewise, the elements that constitute murder (criminal law) are the unlawful killing (without defense) of a human being or a fetus with malice aforethought (planned, knowing the act of murder is a crime). Lawyers are trained to read between the lines, and it's between those lines that lawyers get creative in the prosecution or defense of a particular case.

My study of law at WSU from 1975 to 1978 was like a three-year bar review course since a juris doctor only becomes a license to practice law once the prospective lawyer passes the state bar exam. Passing gives the candidate the opportunity to use *Esq.* (esquire) after his or her name. I took the bar exam in July 1978, and results were posted in November that year, a few days before Thanksgiving. Back then, before the availability of e-mail, the only way to find out if you passed the exam was to drive to downtown Los Angeles where the *Daily Journal*, the legal newspaper read by lawyers and judges, posted the names of the successful candidates on the inside of the huge windows facing the street. It was a Saturday morning, bright and clear, and my then-wife, Leslie, and I piled into our green 1971 Ford Pinto hatchback, with Easha, our Irish setter, in the back. We drove from our home in Anaheim to downtown Los Angeles in total silence. I was in no mood for small talk, and Leslie correctly sensed my mood. She also felt the anxiety of the moment. I can't remember being more nervous about anything prior to that moment, since so much was riding on my passing the exam. I didn't want to have to retake it in February 1979—that would mean another three months of studying and waiting for results that wouldn't be posted until June.

I parked across the street from the *Daily Journal* building, told Leslie to stay in the car, and headed to the crowd of people pushing and shoving toward the front window to look for their names. I wormed my way into the crowd and eventually was facing the list of successful candidates. Many elated people passed by as did many dejected-looking people. I finally got to the front row and ran my finger down the list. In that moment I actually forgot my name! For about ten seconds, I didn't know who I was, but when I finally gained some composure, I looked again. There it was: Mark Roseman. I had passed the state bar exam on my first try, and so had my friends Frank and Mike. That day was one of the happiest and most fulfilling of my life.

In truth, practicing law taught me prison survival skills—though, of course, I couldn't have known that then. Law students are drilled to identify the issues in a set of facts and situations. Once the issue is spotted—was there a contract? Was *A* negligent when he sideswiped *B*'s car? Did *C* and *D* enter into a lease?—a formula for further analysis kicks in that creates a paradigm shift in how one views the world. Dean Boas's words were prophetic. I did learn how to think like a lawyer, and that thinking not only helped me in my career, it helped me to survive.

The law student and the lawyer are trained to identify facts of a case and assess them in relation to the rule of law relevant to the issues presented by the facts. Once a student or attorney identifies the issue and rule of law, he or she does an analysis of the law as applied to the issues raised by the facts. Where there is a dispute about the facts or the correct rule of law, the case ultimately goes to trial or to some other form of dispute resolution. Herein lies the essence of thinking like a lawyer; this is where the analytical minds of trial lawyers, transactional lawyers, criminal defense attorneys, prosecutors, and judges learn to rapidly assess situations through the chess game of pretrial discovery that includes depositions, written interrogatories, and cross-examination of witnesses. The student or lawyer learns to view important issues in every case from all angles in anticipation of the opposing side's view of the same issue. Conclusions on a law school exam normally don't have to be right or wrong but must be carefully and convincingly analyzed. In prison, a conclusion gleaned from these assessments can save your life or put you in jeopardy.

Law school exams and bar examinations test this formula of thinking in civil and criminal law fact patterns known as IRAC: Issue—Rule—Analysis—Conclusion. The IRAC method of thinking eventually became part of my internal thinking code. Talk to a lawyer about any topic that has no obvious answer and eventually you'll stumble into the world of IRAC thinking. To nonlawyers who do not practice such analytical thinking, the method often comes across as legalese, and there is some truth to the adage: "Ask a lawyer the time and be prepared to be told how to build a watch." How the watch is built is often foundational to what time it is in any particular time zone.

The prison environment presented me daily with strange situations that called upon me to use IRAC thinking. For instance, running IRAC in a rat situation went like this:

Issue: would telling a guard that Whiskers told me about his stash of pot in his locker constitute my being a rat (wet or dry)?

Rule: a wet rat gives full details to a guard about another inmate's conduct. A dry rat infers the conduct without naming the inmate involved.

Analysis: wet and dry rats are looked down upon by the general prison population because the information rats provide penetrates the peace of the community and potentially results in other inmates being subject to discipline.

Conclusion: keep the information about Whiskers's pot stash to myself as a means of self-preservation.

All the unwritten rules surrounding surviving the culture shock of prison fit perfectly into the IRAC formula. For example, on the topic of food the formula looks like this:

Issue: I want to share an open bag of corn chips with Copp'r because he is hungry.

Rule: as a wood, I must never share an opened package of food with a black or gay person.

Analysis: the nonsense of the rule did not nullify the essence of the rule, and for self-preservation, I must make a case-by-case determination to usurp the rule—but only under special circumstances when no overt exchange will be detected.

Conclusion: in certain instances I decided to reject the rule, and although I took a chance, I shared food with those I was not supposed to simply because the rule was stupid and only when my self-preservation antennae gave a green light.

Inmates who failed to appreciate the issue at hand were destined to be hurt. Those who did not understand a particular nuance or prevailing lexicon on a particular yard were certain to be preyed upon. An example was someone labeled Maytag thinking he was being equated to a washing machine. Likewise, not knowing and appreciating the racial rules involved in sports, television viewing, and housing arrangements meant an inmate did not know the issues raised by those rules, and this misunderstanding could rapidly escalate into a life-threatening situation.

I entered all new situations in my prison experience with IRAC as my shield and sword. However, I did so carefully, aware that the analysis in prison culture is often unpredictable, knee-jerk, and swift. When Spike realized I was Jewish and ordered me to move my bunk, the IRAC system kicked in:

Issue: should I move my bunk to accommodate the racist hatred of a person who could hurt me?

Rule: skinheads are to be feared due to their blind hatred of Jews.

Analysis: Spike and I were being housed in a cramped, converted former gymnasium at Ironwood. I knew of no other skinheads being housed with us, and I did know of one other large, burly Jew named Mordechai who was housed with us and who had earlier pledged to watch over me to ensure my safety. I believed him.

Conclusion: I told Spike to move, and he did.

In addition to my legal training and the legal skills I honed through hard work and study, I have always been a good listener. Being a good listener is an asset for an attorney and for a prisoner. On the inside, the system and your race and your group affiliations are constantly telling you what to do. Listening without passing judgment is critically lacking, and that void creates stress, anxiety, confusion, and potentially errant behaviors.

Wherever I was housed within the system, word quickly spread that I had been an attorney. That fact became important to men who had no access to the outside legal world. It became clear to me very soon into my incarceration that the prison system provided no access for inmates with civil matters pending on the outside. A guard might call an inmate to a program office only to see him served with legal documents; these ran the gamut from divorce papers (including custody and child support) to paternity suits to probate matters (one inmate, for instance, inherited five thousand acres of land in Texas, but until I interpreted the legalese for him, he had no idea of the significance of the papers he held in his hand). Some inmates were called to the program office to be served deportation papers by the US marshal (notice of an immigration hold pending deportation). This meant that upon completion of the inmate's state sentence, the Immigration and Naturalization Service intended to bring deportation proceedings against him to send him back to his home country. These orders were devastating to those who had served many years in prison and had established families on the outside. In some cases these men did not fluently speak the language of their country of origin.

Prisons have medical clinics on every yard, and I believe they should also have free legal clinics for those facing such civil matters. Of course, inmates lose their civil rights while in prison, but ignoring the fact that life goes on outside in the world of civil matters only compounds the problems men face upon release. Lack of knowledge about what certain legal papers mean and what legal remedies they may have lands too many people in an endless cycle of trouble.

Every day while incarcerated, I used the IRAC system. It was my fallback, and to this day I use it, sometimes unconsciously. I use it to ensure that I am thinking straight, that I am weighing all possibilities before making a decision on any important issue. I can clearly make the connection between being educated in the law, my ability to listen well without being critical, and the IRAC system as the major factors that enabled me to survive prison.

CHAPTER TEN

Transformation

Two Years down today. I remember it well. Dropped off in front of the Orange County Superior Court, hands in pockets—Mom says she's "proud of me"—? Not knowing what to expect, but very calm to surrender myself to the court to go to jail and then to prison. I had no idea what was ahead of me; I was resigned to making the most of it, and that spirit remains kindled in me to this day.

—*Journal entry, October 20, 2005*

I CAN BEST DESCRIBE the result of my personal transformation in two words: mind transplantation. In this book, I have revisited the experiences and living conditions that combined to impact that mind-set. Before I began serving my sentence, I internally lectured myself to embrace the position that prison would not change me; it would not break me. That state of mind was an awkward, motivational power stance against forces that truly scared me. Because I had no idea what being a prisoner would be like, for the first six months of my incarceration, images and thoughts haunted me and triggered episodes of depression. I have in many senses forgotten the weeks and days after my sentencing and before surrendering to the court to begin serving my time on October 20, 2003. That October day, when I was handcuffed and taken into custody, I felt as if I were out of my mind, thrust into a parallel universe defined by uncertainty and fear. Over time those feelings have become blunted, but I know I will never lose them altogether.

Lessons Learned

With the benefit of hindsight, I've come to understand my transformation as gaining profound and new perception. The sudden loss of freedom is brutal, but no one else cares, so like all prisoners, I endured the force of that brutality all alone. What I did not realize in October 2003 was how inevitable it was that my life would change. No one can serve two years in prison without reacting to the experience.

When I went to prison, I saw the change as being only negative. Part of my transformation process was realizing that the challenges I faced resulted in positive changes in me. Ironically, being a prisoner allowed me to discover a healthier, new appreciation of my life, both of interactions between other people and an improved self-concept. Since my release, I have come to realize the profound improvements between my pre- and postincarcerated selves. I now trust my instincts in all social situations. I smell bullshit before the cows leave the barn. I call people on their efforts to distort the truth by using jargon. My tolerance for grandstanding for one's own benefit is zero. With each person I encounter, I mentally test his or her chance of survival in prison.

For example, one day, sometime after I was released, a postprison business partner insinuated I didn't have the guts to pick up the phone and call him to talk about an issue between us. The preprison me would have looked for some middle ground, searching for any opportunity to avoid confrontation. The postprison me, without a moment's hesitation, asked him how he could suggest something so ludicrous to someone who had survived two years in prison. He shot back with "Are you threatening me?" But the only threat I posed was that I was calling him out on his cowardice. Since I left prison, I find identifying, confronting, and containing the cowards easy. I'm able to let a great deal go without experiencing spikes in my blood pressure. After standing in a breakfast chow line in freezing cold for what seemed like hours, standing in line at the market to reach an overly engaging, slow cashier spikes no anxiety like it would have in preprison days.

I'm on good terms with the passage of time. Time fascinates me, a constant that reveals itself in life and death. I'm more aware of how time impacts all of us, all the time. In agriculture, for instance, I'm sensitive to the fact that seeds of all kinds flourish and over time feed people, as well as livestock destined for human consumption. Our human seeds and eggs, likewise, will over time turn into future generations, and those generations will bring peace or war; those human beings will be engaged or indifferent. I'm acutely aware of the way two years changed my outward appearance. In prison, I could not see in the stainless-steel mirrors the way my hair grayed so dramatically; I was not aware of signals from my body telling me to slow down. Prison terms are all about time. They're about time served and time yet to be served. In prison I became not only aware of the passage of time but about time's jargon.

For instance, in prison a *lifer* is doing time against a clock with no hands, a calendar that doesn't turn. Lifers have no date and will probably die in prison. Inmates who serve ten years or more are called *long timers*. And anyone who is serving just a few years, people like me, are doing but a minute of time. If a prisoner's release date is fewer than six months away, he's considered *short, shorty*, or *you ain't got no legs*. Some inmates never fully adjust to incarceration and remain angry and distant; those poor individuals are *letting the time do them*.

Imagine mixing a room with lifers and shorts. What would those interactions be like? Every time Morris Teitlebaum and I were transported to Level III security yards for MAC meetings, I saw this firsthand. I was struck by the openness of the conversation about who was doing how much time. Lifers always referenced their sentences as though they had some imaginary release date in mind. They'd say "when I get out," never "if I get out." In California prisons, rumors about the shortening of sentences due to overpopulation come and go with the regularity of Christmas, without the holiday's joyful traditions. On November 6, 2012, California voters approved Proposition 36,[1] which substantially amended the three strikes law, resulting in actual "when-I-get-out" relief for lifers. I remember feeling elation. But I was housed with young men, men in their twenties, whose lives were impacted by Proposition 36 because, in a nutshell, the law effectively doubled sentences for serious second-felony offenders. If such offenders were convicted of a third serious felony, the mandated prison term would be at least twenty-five years to life. These young men had dead eyes. When I looked at them, I saw shells of human beings trying to fill a bottomless time pit. Other than the temporary suspension of reality induced by television or obsessive masturbation, nothing could soothe them. When once I asked one of these men to please turn down the volume of the television, he didn't even react. His sentence and mine were so different that to him I wasn't even living on the planet he inhabited, and that was true. I wasn't.

Other inmates who had the same dead eyes had three or four decades of time behind them, and because of all that time served, they earned instant respect from others. Inmates with no dates were particularly revered in ways I never understood. The OG who early on advised me to be a ghost and not to let the time do me was one of those kinds of inmates—the kind who take no shit from anyone. Like the administration, OGs believe troublemakers must be dealt with firmly and fast. Being a rat and keeping the yard free of troublemakers causes a clash for some, but the long timers are so connected and wired into yard operations, they always know well in advance if trouble is coming. Much like Jewish *Kapos* (prisoner functionaries) in World War II concentration camps, lifers are spared the standard disrespect shelled out by prison guards, but they are never fully trusted in the constantly shifting world of prison. These inmates are never fully trusted by anyone. They have nothing to lose.

I had limited conversations with men who had served decades of time in prison. These men experienced little happiness in their lives. Some became deeply absorbed in religion, while others dedicated themselves to administrative jobs within the prison hierarchy. For the most part these men treated me with little regard—I had an exit date, and they did not. The exceptions to this rule were usually deeply spiritual men.

Reentry through Closed Doors

The above-named person has been discharged from the jurisdiction of the California Department of Corrections on all existing felony commitments as of this date.

—*My certificate of discharge dated 12-18-06 [13 months after my parole]*

The California Department of Corrections uses the term "all existing felony commitments," a term that implies the released prisoner will offend again somewhere down the line. That red flagging a bad apple permeates the reentry process. While the prize at the end of a term served is freedom, the reality is that discharged inmates, after receiving two hundred dollars cash and one set of clean clothes, are on their own.

If a discharged inmate is a gang member, he will likely return to the gang with the distinction of having done hard time.

> Your successful reentry into the community is our wish. We congratulate you on the discharge of your commitment to the California Department of Corrections.

—*Statement from the CDC 163 (Rev. 11/04), Certificate of Discharge*

The CDC's congratulations and well wishes are, in truth, only a continuum of the window dressing of a heartless system. These sentiments sound good, but they have no real human emotion behind them. The *Brown v. Plata* and *Johnson v. California* cases were breakthrough decisions. These Supreme Court decisions relied upon expert witness testimony about the real living conditions of California's inmates. Both cases took decades of litigation, appeals, and heartache to move the CDC's treatment of its charges into the light of the public arena. Does the general public care? Probably not. People who have no direct or indirect contact with the prison system have little or no interest in what's going on behind closed doors.

In part because incarceration is so brutal, reentry is a mixed bag of joy and fear. Those not members of a gang generally move in with parents or friends or melt into the sea of urban homeless. Inmates have no preparation for successful reentry. Guys about to be paroled talked privately to me about their fears and their distrust of themselves. One of several inmates I stayed in touch with after my release wrote to me answering specific questions in furtherance of research for this book. I asked him what was missing on the streets to keep him from violating parole? He wrote back:

> Well, this time around—nothing was really missing. Only my discernment with how to handle an argument with my wife. I don't even drink so I should never have drank. I'm done with all of that. Last time I paroled—lots of things were missing. I paroled to West Covina, California, where I knew absolutely no one. I have no family in California. I took the bus to the parole office and barely had any $ to even get a room in a dive motel. I didn't have any form of ID, and no one would employ me without one. I had no money, no car, and nowhere to live, yet the parole department expected me to be law abiding.

—*Anonymity requested*

Upon my reentry, I was cushioned from such hardships because while still inside I had figured out how to use the system to my advantage. Inmates are paroled back to the county in which they were convicted and usually return right back into the environment that made them prison-bound. Many return to the poisoned well of drugs and drug-related activity. Since I had nothing to go back to in Orange County—no job, no family, and no future—I successfully petitioned to have my parole transferred to San Diego County where my parents lived. I was also fortunate to find employment within the first week of reentry. I lived with my parents for fourteen months and accumulated enough money to get my own apartment.

During reentry, the difference between having supportive family and not having one is huge. The doors to employment, education, housing, medical and dental care, and mental-health care are closed to many inmates upon release, and it becomes up to the individual being released to the streets to reconstruct his or her life. Far too many don't know where to turn for a hand up or have no one to turn to.

The obstacles awaiting the released ex-con are many and include

- *Psychological adjustment to freedom:* The ex-inmate must establish a mind-set for coping with crowds of people, the fast pace of cars, and the barrage of information available over the Internet and social media. What do you do with all of that speed and information?

- *Return to family:* Often family members will not accept an ex-con into the household. Too many prisoners have estranged spouses, children, and extended families.

- *Finances:* After the two-hundred-dollar cash from CDC, few prisoners know where their next income stream will come from.

- *Employment:* A job search always involves finding some way to explain the gap in your resume.

- *Skills:* Poor or no Internet or computer skills is common, especially for those who have served time for years; inside prisoners have no access to computers or the Internet.

- *Housing:* Landlords require an income history, and many do background checks looking for criminal convictions. For my first apartment, my father had to cosign to guarantee the rent. I was fifty-six years old at the time, and I felt like a child, even as I felt the joy of the freedom of having my own place again.

- *Identification:* Obtaining a driver's license or state-issued ID can prove challenging.

- *Alcohol and drug addiction:* I saw no compassion on the part of prison officials toward those struggling with addiction. Witnessing men going through the pain and suffering of forced withdrawal from heroin became commonplace.

- *Education and training:* In the balance between making a living and continuing with education, the average inmate resorts to making money any way he or she can, often without regard to the legality of an enterprise.

- *Marginalization and social stigma:* When a group or individual within a group is pushed to the *edge* of that group and accorded lesser importance, he or she has been marginalized, and this results in social stigma. The stigmatized person's needs and desires are ignored, and ex-cons fit squarely into this group. The public fears ex-cons, and this fear is stoked by politicians calling for a tough-on-crime platform when standing for reelection.

The Federal Government Weighs in on Reentry

Between 1987 and 2007, some fifteen to twenty million people were arrested on drug charges.[2] The punishments drug offenders face often extend far beyond the prison walls and the parole officer's office. The federal government has increased the odds of failed reentry for ex-felons convicted of drug-related crimes. Congress blocked the path of these people's access to federal benefits and services. Many of the laws passed by Congress during these years negatively impact some of society's most vulnerable and marginalized members: the poor, people of color, and women with children.

The following "double jeopardy" laws have been formulated in the last twenty years as part of the ratcheting-up in the war on drugs:

- The Anti-Drug Abuse Act of 1988, under which local housing agencies and others who supervise federally assisted housing have the discretion to deny housing when any household member uses alcohol in a way that interferes with the "health, safety or right to peaceful enjoyment" of the premises by other tenants, illegally uses drugs, or has been convicted of drug-related criminal activity.[3] People who are evicted or denied housing under the law are cut off from federal housing assistance for three years.

Under this act, one class of drug offender is specifically prohibited from obtaining public housing—persons who have been convicted of manufacturing methamphetamines. They, along with society's other favorite demonized group, registered sex offenders, are the only groups of offenders singled out for prohibitions.

- The 1990 Denial of Federal Benefits Program, which allows state and federal judges to deny drug offenders federal benefits such as grants, contracts, and licenses. According to the US Government Accountability Office (GAO) approximately 600 people a year are affected by this program in the federal courts.[4]

- Section 115 of the Personal Responsibility and Work Opportunity Reconciliation Act of 1996 (more familiarly known as the Welfare Reform Act), under which persons convicted of a state or federal felony offense for selling or using drugs are subject to a lifetime ban on receiving cash assistance and food stamps.[5] Convictions for other crimes, including murder, do not result in the loss of such benefits. Section 115 affects an estimated ninety-two thousand women and one hundred thirty-five thousand children.

The Welfare Reform Act contains a provision allowing states to opt out, although if they fail to act, the lifetime bans remain in effect. In fourteen states where legislators have not acted, drug felons still face the federal ban, even though their sentences may be long-finished and their offenses decades old. But in thirty-six states, legislators have acted to limit the ban in some fashion, allowing drug offenders to get public assistance if they meet certain conditions, such as participating in drug or alcohol treatment, meeting a waiting period, having been convicted for possession only, or other conditions.

- Public Law 104-121, which blocks access to Supplemental Security Income (SSI) and Social Security Disability Income (SSDI) for people whose primary disability was alcohol or drug dependence.[6] This 1996 law replaced a 1972 SSI Drug Abuse and Alcoholism program that allowed people in drug treatment, which was mandatory, to designate a payee to manage benefits to ensure the money would not be used to purchase drugs or alcohol. The Social Security Administration estimates that more than one hundred twenty-three thousand people lost benefits when this law went into effect, while another eighty-six thousand managed to retain them by virtue of age or by being reclassified into a different primary care disability category.

- The 1998 Higher Education Act's (HEA) drug provision (also known as the Aid Elimination Penalty), provides that people with drug convictions cannot receive federal financial aid for a period of time determined by the type and number of convictions.[7] This law does not apply to others with convictions, including drunk-driving offenses, violent crimes, or other criminal offenses. In 1997, the provision was reformed to limit its applicability to offenses committed while a student is enrolled in college and receiving federal aid. Since the law went into effect in 2000, some two hundred thousand have been denied student financial aid.

- The Hope Scholarship Credit, which allows income tax deductions for people paying college tuition and fees.[8] The credit allows taxpayers to take up to a one-thousand-dollar credit for tuition and additional credits for related expenses. It specifically excludes the credit for students who were convicted of a drug offense during the tax year in question or for their parents paying the bills.

While the GAO notes that "thousands of persons were denied postsecondary education benefits, federally assisted housing, or selected licenses and contracts as a result of federal laws that provide for denying benefits to drug offenders," it is low-balling the real figure, which, according to its own numbers, is in the hundreds of thousands. Additionally, the GAO report does not factor in the number of people who simply did not apply for housing, welfare benefits, or student loans because they knew or believed they were ineligible.

Children and the Criminal Justice System

Often, the doors to the prison system are flung open to juvenile offenders, setting the stage for years of misery in prison and eventual reentry through avenues that block personal growth and opportunity. A case in point, from an inmate's written answer to my question: how did you become state-raised?

> I started using meth at 13. By the time I was 14 I was participating in manufacturing it. I hung out with all of my older cousins, homeboys. I was a "good kid."
>
> I took the fall on stuff 'cause (as I was taught) I am a minor, the cops can't do anything but take me home, and a few times that's all they would do is take me home, so that in itself turned me into a monster. You see I feel now that all of my older cousins & homeboys prepared me for prison, made me "Prison Bound" long before I knew it.
>
> I have been down for 4 years. I have 18 months left, honestly the past 5 months have been the only time I have been clean since I started this term.

—*James T., Response, November 7, 2011*

Out of Prison, Deep into Debt

Reentry raises the issue of repayment of civil restitution financial judgments against those who enter a plea bargain to avoid trial. More than twelve years after pleading guilty to six grand theft felony charges to avoid the potential of a fifteen-year prison sentence if convicted on all charges, I am still dealing with this. The California legislature closed the doors on financial reentry for people like me by eliminating the ten-year statute of limitations on the collections of civil judgments for restitution. The law provides no statute of limitations. In July 2015, the California Franchise Tax Board notified me, after nearly twelve years of silence, that it represents the California Department of Corrections and Rehabilitation in the collection of restitution for the full civil judgment to which I pled in September 2003. They are garnishing a monthly payment from my wages against the principal owed. I will be fully paid up when I'm ninety years old.

In addition, each month the California Employment Development Department garnishes money from my pay for back taxes not paid by Blum & Roseman. The monthly payment against the principal owed the state will be fully paid when I'm 107 years old. For me and for so many others across the country, the practice of saddling ex-offenders with crushing debt—debt that the federal government, through the bankruptcy code, does not allow to be discharged—and tag teaming with the states to collect on debts that have little likelihood of being collected is Dickensian.

If a felony conviction is a penalty that keeps making life difficult, if not impossible, because of the many closed doors and legislative obstacles meted out to individuals to keep them relegated to the sidelines of society, we must recognize we have created a society that forever punishes anyone who has been charged with and sentenced to serve time for any offense.

I have experienced transformation and have had transformative realizations from my prison experience. Some were clear to me while I was inside, while others took years to reach consciousness. On October 20, 2003, I realized within minutes of being locked up in OCJ that with incarceration I had entered a dangerous and topsy-turvy world. With no life experience upon which to compare what was happening to me as an inmate, I relied on and learned to trust my animal instincts. On the inside, I operated on instinctual autopilot when confronting situations that became important to me. My nature is to be nonaggressive and to negotiate, but in a confrontational situation, my instincts told me that I could be risking my life if I misread anything. This was, perhaps, the most transformative element I experienced. My confrontation in the library with the skinheads is an example of an instinctual reaction with potentially harsh consequences but one that worked. My instincts instantaneously read the situation when I told a skinhead if he didn't like sharing his lower bunk with a Jew, he should move. Of course, I believed my friend Mordechai had my back since he had told me he would assist me with anything I needed, and still today I can see those perfect Jewish stars he had tattooed on his huge biceps and the Shalom tattooed across his chest in Hebrew.

My basic instincts also informed my interactions with Spike, who got to know me on a deeper level than either of us probably expected he would. I helped him with reading and writing letters from his old lady, and he let me into his life—to a point. When he asked me to take dictation of a letter to a woman, he talked about sex and food, and he said hateful things about other races. I suggested he say something nice to her, but besides talking about how he missed her ass and missed partying with her, he could not tap into any emotional connection to her; that seemed a foreign concept to him.

Another basic animal instinct was my recognizing the sudden change in mood on the yard when something bad was about to happen. It was like having a sixth-sense barometer of the pressure level among inmates. I can liken the feeling best to the way animals react before an earthquake. As a longtime California resident, I've seen housecats become catatonic or run and hide just moments before a seismic event was sensed by human beings. And I've read documented reports of pets vanishing or wildlife disappearing ahead of large earthquakes. Animals, in general, shy away from unpleasant stimuli; one theory has it that a change in the ionization of the air caused by a seismic event triggers animals' behaviors before that event occurs, and that was the sense I sometimes had on the yard—that something was about to happen.

The transformative lessons I learned after prison are many and varied. I came to realize that I am a resilient person who steadfastly overcomes adverse conditions and situations. In that regard, my definition of boredom has changed greatly. Compared to prison life, nothing on the outside comes close. This change of perspective recently kept me calm in a situation that made many others angry and aggressive. On October 16, 2015, I was driving south from the San Francisco East Bay area to Los Angeles to attend a conference in Studio City. The night before, a flash flood had devastated the Grapevine area of the state, resulting in the closing of the Grapevine portion of the Interstate 5. This section is a steep, winding road with a dramatic incline to three thousand feet, but mudslides and flash flooding had closed the area just when I and thousands of others needed to drive over it to reach the Los Angeles basin. Alternative routes were few, and two of those were also washed out. The only passable road going west to connect with southbound State Route 101 was State Route 46.

As I headed west on Route 46, I felt something stir inside me. I was entering the town of Wasco, the town where California's reception prison, the one where I was housed while awaiting transfer to Ironwood, is located. Not long after I had started heading west, I saw the prison compound looming in the distance. I was traveling at the posted speed limit of fifty-five, but I slowed slightly to take it all in. The traffic on Route 46 was slowing anyway, but suddenly I was flooded with memories of being inside that place, and especially memories of feeling bored. Not far down the road, the traffic came to a sudden halt, and I spotted a traffic sign announcing that traffic would be stop and go for the next thirty miles, the distance to Route 101 to Los Angeles. While other drivers and their passengers growled and honked and otherwise showed their fury and frustration and boredom at sitting in this slow-moving traffic jam, I flashed back to my life at Wasco prison and realized that compared to sitting there, I was here. I was in my car, totally free, going somewhere—slowly, yes, but going. Plans had changed only because of a force of nature, not because a guard was locking the door and shouting orders. I felt healthy and fortunate and even happy. My resiliency and healthy perspective changed my perspective altogether. What would have been a two-hour drive but turned into eleven hours still left me smiling all the way to my destination.

Many of my transformation realizations have to do with identifying human behaviors that immediately raise red flags. In business, I don't give the benefit of the doubt to people I don't instinctively trust. In social settings, the same is true. I've learned the real hatred in the prison world is simply a microcosm and a mirror of the outside world. I've looked hatred in the eyes, and now I recognize when I ought to avoid certain people. And I do. I can spot a drug deal going down in a public place the way most people see buildings and trees. I recognize certain movements that are associated with deviant behaviors acquired in prison. Like an animal, I instinctively recognize trouble.

The most personal transformation has been in my spiritual being. Having been raised in the Jewish religion and immersed in the traditions and teachings concomitant with being a Jew, I learned to identify proudly as one. However, my Jewish education was not potent or relevant enough to hold me as a practicing Jew. My first wife, Leslie, kept a kosher home; in those days I was on the board of a synagogue and attended High Holiday services. I have run the Seder at Passover, and I enjoy the culture, food, and music associated with my Jewish upbringing. But as an inmate, it was not my religion that brought me solace and comfort. What got me through was a spirituality that is hard to define, spirituality that is not housed in a building, found in a ceremony, or contained in a specific book or tract. It is housed in me. I now realize that I am a congregation of one, a Jew, without the trappings. Ironically, I became more in touch with my historical Jewish roots while immersed in a culture of anti-Semitism.

Afterword

THE BOOK IN YOUR hands is not the one I originally conceived. Ten years ago, I thought a book of memoirs with stories about prison life would be interesting. I also believed that how and why my experiences transformed me as a person would be helpful to readers who had been through unimagined life experiences but had come out standing. My original view was myopic and too self-centered.

What occurred during the process of writing this book was a more encompassing transformation of thinking than I had anticipated. In a first draft, I specifically wrote that the book was not about prison reform. I intended to include stories and vignettes and to leave it up to the reader to read between the lines and conclude that prison reform was necessary. My stories about overcrowding, poor health care services, dangerous living situations, and state-sanctioned racism, I believed then, as I do now, would speak to the issue of prison reform without my having to underscore the point.

My broader transformation, with the benefit of ten years of perspective and the experience I wrote of reliving my time as an inmate, ignited the advocate in me to forthrightly push for prison reform in California and beyond. Trails of what had become dormant advocacy transformation after my return to the streets were renewed in the writing. In 2006, I became a volunteer with the Texas-based Prison Entrepreneur Program (PEP) and worked long distance with a parolee to put together a moving-van company. The PEP philosophy, taken from its website, is

Prison inmates . . . have a massive reservoir of untapped potential. Their latent potential once expressed itself in illegitimate business endeavors e.g., gang-related crime, drug dealing and violent crime. PEP seeks to redirect these men into legitimate enterprises, leveraging their proven entrepreneurial skill-sets to inspire an even deeper change.

Since becoming a PEP volunteer, I've moved on to become a supporter of locally based prison action reform groups, including the following:

- *Friends Outside:* This national, family-centered organization has branches in the San Francisco area. Its goal is to help former inmates achieve a sense of personal responsibility and productiveness. Friends Outside wants individuals to rediscover their abilities through appropriate interventions and to become self-directed toward positive outcomes.

- *Californians United for a Responsible Budget (CURB):* CURB has a persistent advocacy presence in Sacramento pushing hard throughout the state against more jails, cells, and prison construction, among other endeavors. CURB needs national support to fight against California awarding huge sums of money to build more prisons and jails. On November 2, 2015, the Board of State and Community Corrections (BSCC), a California state agency, recommended distributing a half billion dollars to fund jail construction in fifteen counties. The BSCC will have one final vote to officially approve financing the jail projects. CURB opposes such madness.

- *Pain of the Prison System (POPS:)* I am a volunteer speaker for this organization in the Oakland area. The POPS mission statement is "To provide a safe space for high school students who are struggling with the pain of the prison system and to nourish those students in body and spirit, offering support, community and opportunities for expression." POPS addresses the needs of a population that gets lost in the criminal system and acts affirmatively with programs that uncover the shame of those young people who are punished secondarily to parental and family incarceration. POPS relies upon research that shows that childhood health problems, behavior problems, and grade-retention problems are directly associated with having a parent or caregiver in prison. POPS's model for safe and secure intervention in high schools should be a national model for high school students who are impacted by the prison system and dismissively marginalized in the process. The POPS website also offers an excellent list of organizations that advocate for families and children that are involuntarily drawn into the wake of the prison system, and POPS seeks to bring clubs to schools across the country.

It is my hope that this book has awakened in you the need to more carefully examine what's going on in the prison system in your state. I don't advocate for destruction of all prisons but rather a sane approach to stop filling and refilling them. There are private industry-for-profit prisons in this country that need careful scrutiny. Changes in state and federal sentencing guidelines and meaningful diversion programs to make prison less punitive and more a rehabilitation experience are an imperative in this country.

Transforming from a passive storyteller to an advocate for good causes is my ultimate personal transformation as a result of being an incarcerated felon. Prison, as it turned out, was not a waste of my time.

Notes

Preface

1. Tennessee Williams. *Not about Nightingales* (Sewanee, TN: University of the South, 1998).

2. Brown v. Plata, 131 S.Ct. 1910, 179 L.Ed.2d 969 (2011).

3. Plata v. Brown, 563 U.S. 493 (2011).

4. Philip G. Zimbardo, Christina Maslach, and Craig Haney, "Reflections on the Stanford Prison Experiment: Genesis, Formation, Consequences," in *Obedience to Authority: Current Perspectives on the Milgram Paradigm*, ed. Thomas Blass (New York: Psychology Press, 2000), 217.

5. Philip Zimbardo, PhD, in discussion with the author, April 1, 2015.

Chapter One

1. University of California, Irvine (UCI). The University of California, Irvine Medical Center (UCIMC) is a major research hospital in Orange County, California.

2. Nick Anderson and Esther Schrader, "50 Couples to Get $10 Million to End UCI Fertility Clinic Suits," *Los Angeles Times*, July 19, 1997, Orange County edition.

3. Ibid.

4. Semi Mehta, "Two O.C. Attorneys Accused of Looting Accounts," *Los Angeles Times*, April 27, 2003, Orange County edition.

5. Ibid. Quoted statement by Allan H. Skokke, my attorney for pretrial purposes.

6. Mehta, "Two O.C. Attorneys Accused of Theft."

7. In the Matter of Melanie R. Blum, State Bar Court of the State Bar of California Hearing Department–Los Angeles, Case Nos. 96-O-03531-CEV and 96-O-08111, Decision, filed August 20, 2001. "After considering the

misconduct and balancing the serious aggravation and the absence of miti-
gating circumstances, the Court believes that three years stayed suspension
and three years [sic] probation on conditions including nine months' actual
suspension and continued psychological treatment is sufficient to preserve
public confidence and to maintain high standards for the legal profession"
(p. 13, lines 17–20, to p. 14, line 1).

8. In the Matter of Melanie Rae Blum, Case Nos. 99-O-11705, 99-O-12610,
00-O-10367, 00-O-10558, 00-O-11106, 00-O-11840, 00-O-12339, 00-O-12692
and 01-0-01723, Stipulation as to Facts and Conclusions of Law, October 1,
2001.

9. Ibid., 17–21, signed on page 21 by deputy trial counsel for the state bar,
Melanie, and her second attorney for state bar matters, Joanne Robbins.
"Moral turpitude" requires a certain level of intent, guilty knowledge, or
willfulness. See Sternlieb v. State Bar 52 Cal.3d 317 (1990).

Chapter Two

1. As governor, on May 4, 1970, James Rhodes sent National Guard troops onto
the Kent State University campus, resulting in the shooting deaths of four
students.

2. See California Code of Civil Procedure Sec. 340.1.

3. Ibid.

4. Hearsay evidence is evidence of a statement that was made other than by a
witness at a hearing or trial that is offered for the truth of the matter stated.
Hearsay is not admissible unless it meets an exception to the general rule.
California Evidence Code Sec. 1200. Multiple hearsay (double hearsay) is not
admissible without exceptions provided by law. California Evidence Code
Sec. 1201.

5. In the Matter of Melanie Rae Blum, State Bar Court Hearing Department–Los
Angeles, Case Nos. 90-O-03531-CEV, 96-O-08111, Decision, filed April 20, 2001.

Chapter Three

1. In the Matter of Melanie R. Blum State Bar Court of the State Bar of California
Hearing Department–Los Angeles, Case Nos. 96-O-03531 and 96-O-08111,
Stipulation as to Facts and Conclusions of Law, filed June 28, 2000.

2. Examples of self-serving misrepresentations made by Melanie and adopted
by the state bar court include: "It was after he [the author] took over the
operation of the office that trust account problems began." Ibid., 3D., and
"Roseman instructed office staff not to tell Respondent anything that would
upset her and divert her attention away from the fertility cases which her
partner anticipated would bring a great deal of money." Ibid., 5J.

3. In the Matter of Melanie Rae Blum, State Bar Court of the State of California Hearing Department–Los Angeles, Case Nos. 96-O-03531 and 96-O-08111, Notice of Disciplinary Charges, filed August 12, 1999.

4. In the Matter of Melanie R. Blum, State Bar Court of the State Bar of California Hearing Department–Los Angeles, Case Nos. 96-O-03531 and 96-O-08111, Nolo Contendere Plea to Stipulation as to Facts, Conclusions of Law, filed June 28, 2000, page 1A.

5. Ibid., 4G.

6. Ibid., 4H.

7. In the Matter of Melanie Rae Blum, State Bar's Responsive Brief on Review, Case No. 96-O-03531, filed February 4, 2003, by Charles Weinstein, Deputy Trial Counsel, p. 5, lines 15–16.

8. Ibid., 4, lines 21–23.

9. In the Matter of Melanie Rae Blum, State Bar Court of the State Bar of California, Hearing Department–Los Angeles, Case No. 96-O-03531, Opposition to Motion for Filing Under Seal, filed on or about May 14, 2001, p. 3, lines 12–17.

10. Mark E. Roseman, William B. Craig, and Gini Graham Scott, *You the Jury: Allegations of Sexual Abuse* (Santa Ana, CA: Seven Locks, 1997).

11. In the Matter of Melanie Rae Blum, State Bar Court of the State Bar of California Hearing Department–Los Angeles, Case Nos. 99-O-12610, 00-O-10367, 00-O-10558, 00-O-11106, 00-O-11840, 00-O-12339, and 00-O-12692, Notice of Disciplinary Charges, filed January 4, 2001, p. 2, para. 4.

12. In the Matter of Melanie Rae Blum, State Bar Court of the State Bar of California Hearing Department–Los Angeles, Case Nos. 99-O-12610, 00-O-10367, 00-O-10558, 00-O-11106, 00-O-11840, 00-O-12339, and 00-O-12692, Stipulation as to Facts and Conclusions of Law, filed October 1, 2001, and signed the same day by Melanie.

13. Order of the Court (November 30, 2001), Marriage of Blum v. Roseman, (No. 00-D-005611).

14. The People of the State of California v. Melanie Rose Blum, Mark Elliot Roseman, Notice of Motion to Sever Trials, Superior Court of the State of California, for the County of Orange, filed June 10, 2003 (hearing date June 20, 2003), p. 5, lines 8–20.

15. *Melanie R. Blum*, State Bar Court, Decision. Case Nos. 96-O-03531 and 96-O-08111, filed April 20, 2001, p. 4, lines 8–14.

16. Ibid.

17. Ibid.

18. Ibid.

19. Ibid., lines 15–18.

20. Ibid., lines 21–23.

21. Ibid., lines 15–24.

22. Melanie Rae Blum, State Bar Court, Case Nos. 99-O-12610, 00-O-10367, 00-O-10558, 00-O-11106, 00-O-11840, 00-O-12339, and 00-O-12692, Stipulation, filed October 1, 2001, and signed the same day by Melanie, p. 21.

Chapter Four

1. State of California Department of Corrections and Rehabilitation, Office of the Secretary, *2013 Outcome Evaluation Report*, January 14, 2014, signed by Jeffrey Beard, PhD, Secretary.

Chapter Five

1. I prefer the term *staff member* to *correctional officer*. When I do use the term *correctional officer* or CO in this book, it is not in a literal sense. I was confined by the California Department of Corrections (CDC); the name was changed in July 2005 to the California Department of Corrections and Rehabilitation (CDCR), changed in name only. I never experienced any guard initiate or engage in conduct that would benefit inmates, and there was zero evidence of programs geared toward the rehabilitation of inmates.

2. Johnson v. California, 545 U.S. 162 (2005).

3. Abraham Maslow, American psychologist, 1908–1970. Maslow identified the basic psychological needs of humans as food, water, shelter, oxygen, and sleep.

4. "Once upon a time there was a little boat . . ."

5. Frankl, Viktor E., *Man's Search for Meaning* (New York: Pocket Books, 1984).

6. When I entered the system, the name of the department was "the California Department of Corrections." In July 2005, during the Schwarzenegger administration, the department was renamed "the California Department of Corrections and Rehabilitation." The reference to "rehabilitation" is just so much window dressing.

7. Andras Jauregui, *Huffington Post*, posted August 20, 2015.

8. The Prison Rape Elimination Act (PREA) was passed in 2003 with unanimous support from both parties in Congress. U.S.C. §156014 Title 42, Chapter 147.

9. Dan Morain, "Prisons: Weightlifting Gear Is Being Removed and Some Law Books May Be Next," *Los Angeles Times*, February 9, 1998. "The California Department of Corrections is removing weights that many inmates pump to bulk up muscles. And in an even more fundamental step, the department proposes to take away many of the law books that inmates use to challenge their confinement. . . . 'We got into the position at one juncture of providing

a rather comfortable lifestyle in prison,' said Sean Walsh, Gov. Pete Wilson's spokesman. 'We should not allow prisoners to ride roughshod over the prisons. They're there to be punished, and hopefully rehabilitated. They're not there to be entertained and catered to.'"

10. California Penal Code Sec. 311g also defines "obscene live conduct" as "any physical human body activity, whether performed or engaged in alone or with other persons, including but not limited to singing, speaking, dancing, acting, simulating, or pantomiming, taken as a whole, that to the average person, applying contemporary statewide standards, appeals to the prurient interest and is conduct that, taken as a whole, depicts or describes sexual conduct in a patently offensive way and that, taken as a whole, lacks serious literary, artistic, political, or scientific value."

11. Outside the walls of prisons and jails, an important distinction exists between obscene and nonobscene sexually explicit materials. Obscene materials are not provided with legal protection under the First Amendment, Miller v. California, No. #70-3, 413 U.S. 15 (1973), and therefore their sale and distribution, including dissemination through the mails, may be prosecuted. Inside prisons and jails, such materials may also be barred without running afoul of the First Amendment. The difficulty often arises in determining which materials fit within the legal definition of obscenity, and it is a determination that must be made for each individual publication. To be deemed obscene, under the standard set forth in Miller, a publication, film, or other work, taken as a whole, must appeal "to the prurient interest in sex," portray "in a patently offensive way, sexual conduct specifically defined by the applicable state law; and, taken as a whole," must lack "serious literary, artistic, political, or scientific value."

12. California Code of Regulations Title 15, Section 3007.

13. California Penal Code section 7500.

14. Compared to $22,964 for HIV-positive care for someone on MediCal or $7,966.00 for this population in the AIDS Drug Assistance Program (ADAP).

15. During this same time period, the San Francisco Aids Foundation reported the HIV rate in California's state prison system was nearly eight times that of the general population, with unprotected sex between inmates serving as the primary means of transmission. These new cases, the studies point out, disproportionately affect women and communities of color.

16. Trop v. Dulles, 356 U.S. 86 (1958).

17. Furman v. Georgia, 408 U.S. 238 (1972).

18. Hudson v. McMillian, 503 U.S. 1 (1992).

19. Brown v. Plata, 563 U.S. 493 (2011).

20. Justice Kennedy was joined in the majority decision by Justices Ruth Bader Ginsburg, Stephen Breyer, Sonia Sotomayor, and Elena Kagan. Chief Justice John Roberts was joined in the minority by Justices Antonin Scalia, Clarence Thomas, and Samuel Alito.

21. The Eighth Amendment prohibits cruel and unusual punishments but also mentions "excessive fines" and bail.

22. Brown v. Plata, 563 U.S. 493 (2011).

23. Ibid.

24. Ibid.

25. Ibid.

26. "Brown v. Plata," Oyez, retrieved November 15, 2015, https://www.oyez.org /cases/2010/09-1233.

27. In 2011, Governor Edmund G. Brown Jr. signed Assembly Bill (AB) 109 and AB 117, historic legislation designed to helped California close the revolving door of low-level inmates' cycling in and out of state prisons.

Chapter Six

1. Philip G. Zimbardo, Christina Maslach, and Craig Haney, "Reflections on the Stanford Prison Experiment: Genesis, Transformations, Consequences," in *Obedience to Authority: Current Perspectives on the Milgram Paradigm*, ed. Thomas Blass (Mahwah, NJ: Lawrence of Erlbaum Associates, 2000), 204.

2. Ibid., 205.

3. Bureau of Justice Statistics, NCJ 213133, May 2006.

4. Paul Johnson, *A History of the Jews* (New York: Harper & Row, 1987).

5. Shmoop Editorial Team. "Travels with Charley Race Quotes," Shmoop University, Inc., last modified November 11, 2008, http://www.shmoop.com /travels-with-charley/race-quotes-3.html.

6. Brown v. Board of Education of Topeka, 347 U.S. 483 (1954).

7. Johnson v. California, 543 U.S. 499 (2005).

8. Ibid.

9. "Johnson v. California." Oyez. Chicago-Kent College of Law at Illinois Tech, accessed November 15, 2015, https://www.oyez.org/cases/2003/03-6539.

10. Ibid.

11. Johnson v. California.

Chapter Seven

1. The term *groupthink* was first used by social psychologist Irving L. Janis in 1972.

Chapter Eight

1. Sam Gustin, "Prison Phone Calls Will No Longer Cost a Fortune," *Time*, February 12, 2014, http://www.time.com/6672/prison-phone-rates/.

2. Office of the Inspector General, Special Report: August 2009 Riot at the California Institution for Men, April 2010, California Peace Officers Association, http://www.ccpoa.org/files/cimspecialreport.pdf.

Chapter Ten

1. California Proposition 36 (2000) was the Substance Abuse and Crime Prevention Act of 2000.

2. P. S. Smith, "The Conviction That Keeps On Hurting: Drug Offenders and Federal Benefits Drug War Chronicle," issue 471, February 4, 2007.

3. 21 U.S.C. ch. 20, subch. I § 1501 et seq.

4. Denial of Federal benefits to drug traffickers and possessors, 21 U.S.C. 862.

5. Personal Responsibility and Work Opportunity Reconciliation Act of 1996, 21 U.S.C. 862a, sec. 115.

6. Contract with America Advancement Act of 1996, 5 U.S.C. 601.

7. The 1998 Higher Education Act's (HEA) drug provision, 20 U.S.C. ch. 28 § 1001 et seq.

8. The Hope Scholarship Credit, 26 U.S.C. § 25A(b).

Index

About the Author

ARK E. ROSEMAN, JD, is the executive director of both the Steve Frankel Group, LLC (www.sfrankelgroup.com), which provides continuing education courses for mental health professionals, and Practice-Legacy Programs (www.practice-legacy .com), which prepares continuity-of-care plans for mental health practices.

Born in Brooklyn, New York, Mark graduated from the Ohio State University with a bachelor of science degree in agriculture. After completing his undergraduate and postgraduate studies at Ohio State, he graduated from the Western State University College of Law in Fullerton, California. He was admitted to the California bar in 1978. Originally a solo practitioner, Mark became a civil litigation partner with a law firm in Santa Ana, California. In 1987, he and then-wife Melanie Blum formed the law firm of Blum & Roseman.

He became a tenacious advocate for survivors of childhood sexual abuse in 1990—a time when the national conversation on the topic was hushed and subdued. Mark was a member of the task force that drafted the first delayed-discovery statute in California to extend the statute of limitations for survivors of childhood sexual abuse to sue for damages in civil court. He lobbied in Sacramento for the passage of the law he helped draft, Code of Civil Procedure Section 340.1, extending the statute of limitations for locating childhood predators and enabling survivors access to the courts from age nineteen until age twenty-six.

Mark was an executive board member of Mothers Against Sexual Abuse, a national organization founded in 1992 by Claire Reeves, CCDC. Mark also volunteered as the national legal counsel for Linkup, founded in Chicago in 1993 by the late Fr. Tom Economus to bring empowerment and emotional support to survivors of clergy sexual abuse.

Mark is also the coauthor of *You the Jury: Allegations of Sexual Abuse*, which followed a fictionalized case of childhood sexual abuse and asked readers to decide the guilt or innocence of the defendant.

Mark's other professional achievements include serving as a temporary judge, serving as an arbitrator, being coauthor of mental-health-and-the-law articles, and being lead counsel on published California cases on legal issues pertaining to sexual abuse litigation.

You can contact Mark via the following:

Website: http://markeroseman.com
Twitter: @MarkERoseman
Facebook: http://bit.ly/2btiEjI